G000162399

WHEN—Questions for Catholicism

WHEN—Questions for Catholicism

Women, Homosexuality, Ecumenism, and Non-Ordained

MICHAEL J. TKACIK

WIPF & STOCK · Eugene, Oregon

WHEN—QUESTIONS FOR CATHOLICISM
Women, Homosexuality, Ecumenism, and Non-Ordained

Copyright © 2022 Michael J. Tkacik. All rights reserved. Except for brief quotations in critical publications or reviews, no part of this book may be reproduced in any manner without prior written permission from the publisher. Write: Permissions, Wipf and Stock Publishers, 199 W. 8th Ave., Suite 3, Eugene, OR 97401.

Wipf & Stock
An Imprint of Wipf and Stock Publishers
199 W. 8th Ave., Suite 3
Eugene, OR 97401

www.wipfandstock.com

PAPERBACK ISBN: 978-1-6667-3851-3
HARDCOVER ISBN: 978-1-6667-9933-0
EBOOK ISBN: 978-1-6667-9934-7

MAY 26, 2022 2:27 PM

For Suzy

My sun and words, my prophetess and love,
my greatest champion and support, my grace
and source of my courage.

. . . You surpass them all . . . (Proverbs 31:29)

CONTENTS

Acknowledgements

As I share throughout the pages of this work, this book was not easy to write. I would not have had the courage, fortitude, and perseverance to do so if it were not for a plethora of people who, each in their own way, inspired me, affirmed and supported me, and loved me throughout the project.

I will forever be grateful for the gift that the late Fr. Tom McGonigle, O.P., is in my life. All that Tom did was animated by the love of God which radiated forth from him. Never have I encountered a person possessing such a pastoral disposition as Tom. Tom always strived to meet people where they were at and to provide them an encounter with the love of God. Tom's example of love, inclusiveness, and openness to what the Spirit might be saying left an indelible mark on my own theological considerations and pastoral efforts. This book would not have ever come to be if not for his impact upon me.

My university undergraduate religion professor, Dr. Richard Penaskovic, has remained a mentor, colleague, and friend ever since my undergraduate days. Richard has been a constant source of support and trusted friend throughout the years. Dr. Penaskovic has always witnessed to me one who earnestly strives to make theology and the church better, balancing engagement with the tradition vis-à-vis fidelity to the gospel and a prophetic openness to the Spirit which may call for change. I appreciate the time Richard took to review my working draft of the book and for the sound feedback he provided.

Dr. Vance Morgan and Mrs. Jeanne DiPretoro, beloved friends and colleagues, not only reviewed the manuscript and offered excellent recommendations, but have also afforded me a circle of spiritual kinship for some 25 years. The love, trust, and openness to "Big Bird" shared among us has yielded tremendous growth in spiritual awareness and insight which has, in turn, done much to facilitate my growth and maturation as a person of faith. Vance and Jeanne have not only affirmed, loved, and supported me over the years, but have also challenged me to ever become who the Spirit wants me to be.

Reverend Joshua Gyson of All Saints, a Florida based parish within the Evangelical Lutheran Church of America, not only read the draft of the manuscript but also afforded me periodic times of lunch fellowship to not only discuss the book, but to also minister to my soul as I struggled internally with the project. One of the most gifted preachers whom I have ever been fortunate to hear on a regular basis, Pastor Josh has embodied for me and my family an ecumenical openness unparalleled in my experience as a Christian. I will remain forever grateful to Pastor Josh for his friendship and the welcome he afforded me into his ministry, the life of his parish, and at the Lord's Table at which he presided.

Former graduate students, now deacons, the Reverend Joseph P. Mullin, Jr. and Reverend Joseph Bellissimo, emerged from their time as students of mine to become Emmaus brothers. Deacon Mullin read the draft manuscript and provided meticulous feedback. Deacon Bellissimo also read the manuscript and offered constant prayer, affirmation, support, and encouragement throughout the writing process. Respectively and together they rekindled in me a passion for teaching and left me filled with gratitude for the vocation that God has blessed me with. They fill me with hope and inspire me to be the best teacher and scholar that I might be.

My dear *Anawim* . . . a group of very special young women and men who have been my students over the years . . . have inspired me by their love for God, commitment to serve the church, and perseverance in faith. The church moves toward being the best it can be because you so generously give of yourselves as directors of religious education, directors of youth ministry, Catholic school teachers, missionaries, counselors, and the priesthood. Thank you for all that you shared with me and for teaching me about Christian discipleship. It was you who I frequently had in mind as I was moved to give voice to what is proffered in the pages of this book.

Long before I understood the theological importance of equality, inclusiveness, acceptance, and openness to diversity and plurality, my parents and grandmother created a community marked by such for my two sisters, my brother, and me. My family provided me with a true experience of the "domestic church" by exhibiting faith in action. Because of this formative experience, I have been equipped with a knowledge of the gospel and the principles of Catholic social teaching, and afforded a community of faith in

ACKNOWLEDGEMENTS

which they were lived out. Thanks to my family I have known the love of
God and I have known that I am loved precisely as and for who I am, and
that my unique gifts are welcomed and celebrated.

My sons, Charles, Benjamin, and Samuel, and my daughter-in-law
Emily, by both their questions and their lived witnesses, illuminate for me
what a community of faith which treats women with equality, respects persons no matter what their sexual orientation or gender identification, is
open to expressions of truth wherever they are to be discovered, and made
up of persons who possess a healthy sense of their own authority, can be. I
pray that each of you may come to find a community of faith which proves
to be intelligible, meaningful, relevant, viable, and life-giving to you . . . and
one in which your gifts, competencies, and expertise are welcomed, valued,
and allowed to make a difference.

Lastly, a special thanks to Suzy for her constant support and for the
significant amount of time and herculean effort she devoted to readying the
manuscript for publication.

INTRODUCTION

UNEXPECTED EMOTIONS

I WAS CAUGHT OFF guard by a flood of emotions while writing this book. The impact of this writing experience was powerful and unexpected. Although I pondered and prayerfully discerned composing this work for some time, I nonetheless found the process of researching and writing it quite emotionally tumultuous and painful. This is not because I am not convicted that its contents need to be voiced—I am convicted. Rather, it is a type of pain born out of having to challenge the institution I love and have served since I was fourteen years old. Ever since Catholic high school I have dedicated my life to the study of theology and service of the church. I have always experienced my studies and ecclesial service as a vocation. My vocation has been in response to a powerful and palpable call from God to serve God and the Roman Catholic Church through academic studies of theology and philosophy, and by teaching in Catholic colleges/universities. This is what I have done over the past thirty years. Hence, to challenge the church, even if such a challenge stems from my convictions regarding God as I have come to understand, know, and experience God (a gratuitously loving, merciful, forgiving, and accepting God who desires to be in relationship with each and all persons), and one born out of a sincere desire for the church to be the best it can be, it is nonetheless a challenge which is emotionally difficult. It is an experience comparable to having to tell your mother, whom you love, that she is wrong, or that she can and needs to do better. It is an experience which illuminates that, regarding certain issues, the gap between yourself and the one you love is widening.

Theological, Ecclesial, and Cultural Sensitivities

My emotions were additionally heightened due to the vocational and theological sensitivities that inform and provide the framework for how I understand myself as a theologian and teacher. I take seriously the notions of apostolic succession and tradition which underpin and are to strengthen Christian theology. I also take seriously the charisms the Holy Spirit affords the Christian community to illuminate the apostolic deposit of faith. These charisms, in turn, inspire ever new and reformed ways and means to express this faith. Such perennial reform is necessary to ensure the intelligibility, reception, and viability of the faith throughout the epochs of history and plethora of cultural contexts which people find themselves in.[1] As a Catholic, I believe that such charisms are afforded to the church hierarchy (bishops and pope) to preserve and to perpetuate the apostolic faith.[2] However, Catholic theology also recognizes that all of the non-ordained faithful (laity)—the *sensus fidelium*—are afforded charisms from the Spirit to do so as well.[3] This includes women, homosexuals, and non-Catholics. Therefore, in espousing and calling for the acknowledgement and affirmation of the laity's charisms pertaining to teaching authority and the sacramental economy, I am not denying the charisms, nor offices, of the hierarchy. Ecclesial governance and decision making and the sacramental economy are "both/and," not "either/or," when it comes to charisms of the hierarchy and the laity.

The problem, however, is that historically and in practice the Catholic hierarchy has largely functioned in ways that suggest that it alone possesses and exhausts such charisms pertaining to the deposit of faith and apostolic succession. This has lent to clerical monopolization of the sacramental life. Historically and in practice the Catholic Church has been devoid of formal institutional structures and mechanisms and sacramental praxis which allow for and facilitate the charisms the non-ordained possess together with the hierarchy in matters pertaining to the deposit of faith, apostolic succession, and sacramental life. The laity have been marginalized from sacramental praxis and authoritative ecclesial decision making. They have been subordinated to the hierarchy, deprived of their rightful places and roles within the sacramental economy and ecclesial governance as members of

---

1. *Gaudium et Spes*, secs. 58, 44, 62, 53, 31.

2. *Lumen Gentium*, secs. 18–27; *Christus Dominus*, secs. 2–15.

3. *Lumen Gentium*, sec. 12.

the *sensus fidelium*. Such places and roles of the laity are rightfully theirs not only because of the spiritual gifts they possess, but also in light of and by virtue of the places and roles the Lord appoints them by baptism. Via baptism the laity are empowered to share in the three-fold dignity of Jesus as priest, prophet, and king.[4] Historically and in practice, at best the laity have been granted ecclesial structures, mechanisms, and vehicles within the Catholic Church which are deprived of any real authority and substantive import. Such structures, mechanisms, and vehicles have been consistently relegated to mere consultative status, and most exist and function contingently per the discretion of clergy. Additionally, historically and in practice the laity have been largely assigned to passive roles within the sacramental life of the church.

The scenario described above is particularly problematic in cultural contexts where the laity are as educated, or more educated, than the clergy, and within cultural contexts where participatory and democratic forms of governance are taken for granted. Furthermore, in places where ecclesial scandals have rocked the church, the exclusive claim to ecclesial governance and sacramental presidency by the hierarchy has been undermined. The deficiencies in ecclesial governance and sacramental praxis which partly resulted from the laity having no place or role within said governance and sacramental economy have come to be painfully illuminated. The church's own magisterial documents over the past sixty years have identified participatory and democratic forms of governance to be most consistent with the dignity of the human person. As herald of the gospel, the church is to be the greatest champion of human dignity.[5]

Furthermore, since the Second Vatican Council, the baptismal dignity of the laity and its corresponding implications for sharing in the church's priestly (sacramental), prophetic (teaching), and kingly (authority) ministries have been consistently enunciated by the magisterium. Therefore, the church's own teachings regarding human dignity, the *sensus fidelium*, baptism, and governance marked by participation, democratic means, and subsidiarity are compromised and rendered duplicitous and disingenuous if the church, itself, fails to honor and enact that which it calls for.

---

4. *Lumen Gentium*, secs. 31, 33.

5. *Gaudium et Spes*, secs. 31, 68, 73, 75; John Paul II, *Centesimus Annus*, sec. 46; Paul VI, *Octogesima Adveniens*, secs. 22, 24.

A Father and Teacher

The experiences I had while working on this book were also spawned by a sense of love and responsibility that I have for my three sons and my students. They represent the present and future church. For my sons and the majority of my students, a church which does not honor their dignity, baptismal rights and duties, and places and roles within the church as members of the *sensus fidelium*, is unacceptable. This is particularly so given their level of education, cultural experiences and, most importantly, their understandings of God and Jesus. A church which excludes them from authentic decision-making processes and sacramental presidency is unacceptable. A church that marginalizes, subordinates, and patronizes women is unacceptable. A church which is duplicitous in pastoral language regarding homosexuality and condemnatory of homosexual relationships is unacceptable. A church which is not ecumenically inclusive is unacceptable. The Catholic Church will lose many if the church fails to heed and take them seriously.

At a dinner with my diocesan bishop while I was working on this book, the bishop lamented to me and my theology department colleagues that for every one new member being baptized into the church, six members were leaving the church. Trajectories of ecclesial departure are even more marked among younger persons. The bishop asked us how we might address this ecclesial crisis. I think the church could start by being faithful to its own teachings regarding human dignity, participatory and democratic forms of governance, subsidiarity, the *sensus fidelium*, baptismal dignity, ecumenism and inter-religious affairs, and by being more inclusive, accepting, and empowering of women and LGBTQ+ persons.

Over the course of my thirty years of teaching theology at Catholic institutions the majority of my students and majority of theology academic majors and minors have been women. This is in spite of the fact that throughout my years of teaching I have taught specific all male cohorts of deacon candidates within the Catholic Church for six different dioceses on a regular basis. It is experientially clear to me that it is young women who are the increasingly theologically educated in our American ecclesial context. Additionally, it is young women who represent those most interested in serving and remaining engaged with the church. These young women are theologically educated about church teachings regarding human dignity, the *sensus fidelium*, and baptism. They are also a product of a culture which takes democratic and participatory forms of governance and the principle of subsidiarity for granted. Therefore, they, in turn, will rightfully expect more from the church in terms of heeding their "feminine genius" and allowing them authentic instruments and vehicles within the church's structures to participate in real, meaningful, and authoritative ways in ecclesial decision making and the sacramental economy. These women recognize that many women religious are as theologically educated as male members of the hierarchy, yet remain largely jettisoned from ecclesial curial offices, and they rightfully deem such a scenario unacceptable.

I believe that if the church continues to marginalize, subordinate, patronize, and jettison women to secondary status and to the sidelines of ecclesial authority and sacramental praxis, the trajectory of exodus from the church will only increase among young, educated women of America. I have been moved to speak out to challenge the church's attitude and disposition towards and treatment of women. The experiences of the young women I teach are facets and aspects which inform my emotional unsettledness. I have been awakened to the sense of pain and frustration they feel as thoughtful, faithful, and educated members of the church who feel called by God to serve the church but are impeded from doing so by current ecclesial disciplines and praxis which exclude them from ordination, sacramental presidency, and ecclesial governance.

My sons have been raised in both the Roman Catholic and Lutheran (Evangelical Lutheran Church in America) Churches. Together with my wife, we have exposed our sons to both traditions and have striven to empower them to see the riches as well as the shortcomings inherent in both. It is our hope that they may, with the Spirit's help, come to see and experience Christianity in the breadth of its potential and promise, and to discern for themselves what a life-giving expression of the faith ought to look like in practice. Although I do not hold up what we have done as an example or model to be emulated by others, I do not regret raising the boys as we have. Their experiences have afforded them exposure to divergent ecclesial approaches to women, LGBTQ+ persons, ecumenism, and the non-ordained. They have witnessed firsthand a Christian tradition in which women can be ordained, preside at Eucharistic celebrations, and hold hierarchical/episcopal positions. And they have witnessed firsthand a Christian tradition which does not allow for the ordination of women, nor for women to preside at Eucharistic celebrations, and which excludes women from all hierarchical/episcopal positions. Our sons have been members of a Christian community which accepts homosexuality and homosexual relationships, and members of a Christian community which deems homosexual orientation morally neutral but condemns homosexual relationships. Our sons have lived the ecumenical potential of the church, as well as experienced the ecumenical limitations of the church. One church has welcomed them to the Lord's Table of Eucharistic fellowship even as they worship in two different Christian traditions. The other church discouraged them from Eucharistic table fellowship because they worship at the church of their mother as well as of their father. They have seen and participated in a Christian tradition which allows, enables, and empowers them to share in the decision making of the church (at the local parish, national, and global levels), and one which does not.

I believe that their experiences have afforded them both the best and worst of my wife's and my respective Christian traditions. Their experiences have afforded them a healthy and informed understanding of the two respective traditions. From the two traditions they have formulated their own respective understandings of what the Christian community ought to look like if faithful to the example of Jesus.

Part of my pain in writing this book comes from certain aspects of my sons' experiences and upbringing which have brought into focus for me how my Catholic tradition has communicated to them an experience of Christianity that marginalizes, subordinates, and patronizes women; condemns homosexual relationships; and is duplicitous in matters of ecumenism and the non-ordained. Such witness is inconsistent with the gospel and fails to model the example of Jesus. This is not to say that the Catholic tradition has not also provided them important and necessary notions of apostolic succession, tradition, hierarchical charisms, and the irrevocable commitment of Christians to the cause of ecumenism. It certainly has. While Lutheranism illuminated ecclesial subsidiarity in practice by its enabling and empowering of the non-ordained in ecclesial decision making, it has also illuminated the value and importance of hierarchical charisms operative within Roman Catholicism. Whereas, experientially, Lutheranism has afforded them a lived experience of ecumenical inclusivity, Roman Catholicism has provided a magisterial theological sophistication aimed at informing ecumenism.

It is not my intention to pit one tradition against the other, nor to juxtapose them in order to make a case that one is right and the other wrong. Rather, our family experience lends to my own personal pain and reasons for writing this book and informs the challenges and encouragement that

I strive to voice. I also write because I know of many other families whose experience is not unlike our own. I wish for the church to be the best it can be for my sons, for my students, for young people, for all of us.

THE SIGNS AND MARKS OF THE CHURCH, INCULTURATION, AND PNEUMATIC CORRECTIVES

I am writing within the contemporary American context. The Roman Catholic Church has the arduous task of addressing each and all of the myriad of cultures which comprise the global church. To be catholic—universal—devoid of inculturation would be impossible. Inculturation entails the church engaging the diverse and pluralistic experiences of all of the people whom it serves. Without inculturation the faith is not rendered meaningful, relevant, viable, and life-giving. As the Second Vatican Council maintained, inculturation must be the perennial law of evangelization. And as Pope John Paul II conveyed, a faith that is not inculturated is a decapitated faith, a faith in the process of self-annihilation.[6] To be catholic—universal—is to be apostolic, i.e., diverse, pluralistic, and open to inculturation. Apostolicity and catholicity are signs/marks of the church. Yet, the church is also one. Hence, ecclesial unity—oneness—must allow for catholicity—universality—and, thus, allow for apostolicity—diversity, plurality, and inculturation.

Embracing an ecclesial unity unto diversity will be particularly challenging for the Roman Catholic Church. Historically, it deemed ecclesial unity a matter of conformity to a singular Western cultural paradigm and theological methodology and considered ecumenism only to the extent that it called for the return of all other Christians to union with the papacy. Ecclesial unity unto diversity will demand and require humility and trust in the Holy Spirit. It will require understanding unity—ecclesial oneness— more broadly as a unity in Christ as the head of the church in all of its variant, diverse, and pluralistic cultural and religious expressions. Indeed, what the Spirit might be calling the church to do and be in one particular cultural context might be different from that in another cultural context.

> In concrete situations and taking into account of solidarity in each person's life, one must recognize a legitimate variety of possible options. The same Christian faith can lead to different commitments. The church invites all Christians to take up the double task

6. John Paul II, *Ex Corde Ecclesia*, sec. 44; *Gaudium et Spes*, secs. 44, 53, 31, 58.

of inspiring and of innovating, in order to make structures evolve, so as to adapt them to the real needs of today.[7]

Furthermore, what the Spirit asked of the church in a particular historical epoch and/or cultural context may no longer be being asked by the Spirit in the contemporary ecclesial experience and/or in a particular cultural context. Ecclesial unity unto diversity may require acts of *kenosis* (self-sacrificial, self-emptying love) on the part of the church as it adapts and identifies which teachings and structures continue to give life in the contemporary situation and let go of the old which do not. In the work, *Pneumatic Correctives: What is the Spirit Saying to the Church of the Twenty First Century?*, we suggested that, at times, the Holy Spirit calls for a pneumatic corrective:

> As a pilgrim church, the Roman Catholic Church must come to embrace the fact that she is subject to the historical demands and conditions of the times, and that she must adapt and modify herself accordingly so as to be as effective in her mission as possible (*Lumen Gentium,* section 48, and *Gaudium et Spes,* sections 39, 40, and 57) . . .

The church must come to see itself and its teachings are conditioned and limited by the cultural and historical situation in which it finds itself. Ongoing adaptation and renewal must be the primary ecclesial principle. Certain structures and teachings which met the needs and illumined questions of prior ages may no longer be relevant to the contemporary situation.

Consequently, these teachings and structures which do not communicate the faith or truth to contemporary people must be recast so as to address modern needs and questions. The truths of the Christian faith are neither absolute nor relative in their expression, rather they are pneumatic, i.e., they are formed and guided by the Holy Spirit in their meaning and interpretation.[8]

I believe that within the contemporary American Catholic Church the challenges voiced in this work are pneumatic correctives necessary to inculturate the teachings of the gospel within the contemporary American ecclesial experience. However, I also recognize that some of the issues presented in the work would not be culturally compatible with a number of other Catholic communities within the global church. Hence a challenge

---

7. Paul VI, *Octogesima Adveniens,* secs. 50, 4.

8. Tkacik and McGonigle, *Pneumatic Correctives,* 2–3.

that presents itself is a challenge of preserved unity/oneness within the church. Can unity/oneness allow for and embrace diverse cultural expressions of the faith and ecclesial praxis?

I maintain that the sign/mark of apostolicity reveals that such unity unto diversity is possible. Such was the unity experienced and embraced by the apostolic communities themselves. This is evidenced by the diverse narrative accounts of the gospels. The respective gospels present Jesus in different ways in light of the cultural contexts of the communities composing them. Also, pluralistic communal experiences are attested to by the Pauline letters which addressed divergent issues, questions, and practices given varying lived experiences of the respective recipients.

The founding apostolic pillars, Peter, Paul, and James, at the Council of Jerusalem recorded in Acts 15 and Galatians 2, agreed to disagree in terms of moral conduct and ecclesial praxis while simultaneously recognizing and affirming a fundamental unity/oneness of the faith under the headship of Jesus. Diverse practices associated with almsgiving, circumcision, and diet would be tolerated amongst differing cultural contexts which the fledgling church found itself in. These diverse practices were not deemed as compromising the unity and oneness of faith of the various churches under the headship of Jesus. The contemporary church will have to emulate this unity unto diversity if the challenges voiced in this work are to be addressed. Ecclesial practices and positions regarding women and LGBTQ+ persons may initially have to be diverse and pluralistic within the one unified church. What is culturally warranted in one ecclesial setting might not yet be pastorally warranted in another ecclesial setting. However, if proven to be authentic pneumatic correctives, the challenges voiced within the work will eventually need to be implemented throughout the global church. If something is authentically from the Spirit, then the church must embrace and implement it.

Another dimension of my emotional angst in researching and writing this work is concern about the possibility of ecclesial schism. Jesus' prayer in John 17 is that the church be one. As a Christian theologian of conscience, I in no way wish to see the church, the body of Christ, dismembered by schism. Nor, however, do I wish the church to continue to perpetuate injustices toward women, LGBTQ+ persons, the non-ordained faithful, and other people of faith and good will. Fidelity to the Spirit, respect for the dignity of all human beings, and justice, trump concerns of schism. If what the Spirit is saying to the church of the twenty first century is a call to empowering women, accepting homosexual relationships, to advancing the cause of ecumenism and interfaith respect, and empowering the non-ordained, then the answer to the question of "when" is "now." As Dr. Martin Luther King, Jr. voiced in the face of once accepted racial bias, prejudice, and discrimination within the context of the American civil rights movement, when one is experiencing marginalization, subordination, discrimination, and oppression, the answer is not "wait," for "justice delayed is justice denied."[9] When? Now.

As I researched this book, the Methodist Church was in the midst of an ecclesial consideration of unity unto diversity over the very issue of homosexuality.[10] Wishing to avoid schism, yet sensitive to certain divergent cultural understandings of what the Christian faith calls for vis-à-vis homosexuals, the Methodist Church was considering whether or not a fundamental Christian ecclesial unity via faith in and under the headship of Jesus can allow for and tolerate diversity of ecclesial teachings and praxis regarding homosexuality. As was the case among Peter, Paul, and James, the Spirit might be saying to the contemporary church that we might have to agree to disagree on certain teachings and practices. Such disagreement, however, need not forfeit a common fidelity to the gospel, nor surrender an ecclesial unity and oneness under the headship of and faith in Jesus.

The contemporary Catholic Church understands itself to be missionary by nature (*Ad Gentes Divinitus*, section 2) sent out to all people so as to be a sacrament of Jesus pointing to and making present the salvific love of God (See *Lumen Gentium*, sections 9, 13, 16, 17, and *Gaudium et Spes*, sections 42 and 45). Such an ecclesial self-awareness demands that the church respond to "the joys and hopes, the griefs and anxieties of people of this age" (*Gaudium et Spes*, section 1) in a manner that sheds light on how the life, death, and resurrection of Jesus provide meaning to the life experiences of all persons. In imitation of Jesus, the church is to serve all and to show a preferential option towards those who experience marginalization and oppression of any kind.

The gospels testify to Jesus' preferential option for and inclusion of those who were marginalized and oppressed, including women and persons accused of sexual impropriety. Furthermore, the gospels speak of the utter gratuity of Jesus' love, mercy, and forgiveness. Jesus does not spend time speaking of penises, vaginas, gender, orders, or offices. He speaks of

9. King, *Letter from Birmingham Jail*, 3.
10. Briggs, "Methodists may set agree-to-disagree model."

relationships and service marked by the love of God which draws people together with one another and with God. The time to imitate Jesus' acceptance, inclusion, and empowerment of women is now. The time to focus on the complexus of human relationships and human sexual intimacy in light of the whole person and not just anatomical body parts and physiological functions is now. The time to empower the non-ordained, as Jesus did, is now (Neither Jesus nor the disciples were priests. The gospels provide no evidence that the apostles were ordained, were called priests, confected the Eucharist, or exercised authority unilaterally and apart from and uninformed by the lived experience of the people whom they served). The time to embrace the Pentecost lesson of universal inclusion of all peoples (Acts 2) and to acknowledge in praxis that "God shows no partially, rather at all times and in every race, anyone who fears God and does what is right has been acceptable to God" (Acts 10:35) is now. When? Now.

The Goal and Structure of the Book

It is my sincere hope that this work might be a source of comfort for those struggling with the issues in the church pertaining to women, LGBTQ+ persons, ecumenism (and interreligious dialogue), and the laity (non-ordained). To do justice to the teachings of the church, a degree of theological engagement is necessary. At times, working through the church's teachings may prove to be challenging given the nature of theological sophistication employed by the church's magisterium (teaching office). Therefore, I will provide real life stories drawn from my experience in each of the chapters to put a human face on the issues considered. I invite you, the reader, to also think of your own stories, experiences, and loved ones who have been impacted by the church's position on the issues. Although the work entails theological exercise, its goal is ultimately pastoral. An understanding of the church's theological underpinnings for what it teaches is necessary. Honest disagreement can only come if one earnestly strives to understand the position of the other. Possible theological alternatives can only be credible if alternative interpretations can be articulated, or vulnerabilities in the position of the other illuminated. Ultimately, the goal is help those who struggle, as I struggle, with these issues. And, even more so, to convey to women, LGBTQ+ persons, people of other faiths, and the laity that they are rightful members of the church loved by God and endowed with gifts of the Spirit meant to build up the church. Therefore, if or when the theological considerations prove challenging, push on. Push on for the sake of those who experience subordination, marginalization, and pain because of the church's positions on these issues.

I

WOMEN

AN ENVISIONED FUTURE MAGISTERIAL DOCUMENT ON WOMEN

Scripture attests and the Catholic Church affirms that in the beginning God created human beings in God's own image and likeness. Indeed, according to the creation narratives recorded in the book of Genesis, it is only after the initially created earth creature receives a helpmate that the two are differentiated in terms of male and female and furthermore, only then deemed to be the image and likeness of God. Hence, both male and female are the image and likeness of God. The original female, Eve, stands within the biblical narrative as the paradigmatic primordial mother of all. Hebrew Scripture prolifically bespeaks of the role of women within God's providential designs regarding the unfolding of salvation history.

Women such as Sarah, Rebekah, Miriam, Deborah, Ruth, Hannah, Esther, Judith, and a plethora of others are utilized by God to advance the saving designs of God's wisdom and salvation. The sapiential writings of the Hebrew Scripture present Lady Sophia as a personification of God, co-eternal with God, coming forth from the mind of God to mediate between God and human beings, offering to humanity wisdom, light, truth, and the way to God. In short, women are presented in the Hebrew Scriptures as agents of God's wisdom and as mediators of God's saving designs for humanity. Women are presented as acting in the place and on behalf of God on behalf of the community of faith thereby advancing salvation history and humanity's relationship with God.

In the New Testament women are also presented as being instrumental in God making Godself known to humanity. Mary, the mother of Jesus, ensures, by her magnificent fiat, that God's saving designs of salvation via the Incarnation of God's son, Jesus, facilitated by God's Holy Spirit, will occur. Women such as Mary Magdalene, Joanna, Susanna, Mary and Martha of Bethany, Prisca, Lydia, and Phoebe are present throughout the ministry of Jesus and/or play instrumental roles in the preservation and perpetuation of the apostolic faith as the fledgling church emerges and expands. Such women are oftentimes presented as providing for Jesus' ministry and as participating in apostolic missions. They help in establishing early ecclesial communities and serve leadership roles therein.

Indeed, it was women who were entrusted with the central mysteries of the Christian faith. Mary with the birth of Jesus. Mary, Mary Magdalene, and Mary of Clopas were present at the cross at the time of Jesus' crucifixion. And Mary Magdalene was the first to witness the resurrected Jesus, becoming the apostle to the apostles by being sent by the risen Jesus to declare to the others that he had risen.

The Christian tradition honors and reveres the early witness of women virgins and martyrs such as Perpetua and Felicitas, Agape and Irene, and Agnes, upon whose blood and sacrifices the church is built. Numerous women, such as St. Clare of Assisi and St. Scholastica, founded female monasteries and religious orders. St. Catherine of Sienna and St. Teresa of Avila are noted as doctors of the church for their significant contributions to theology and mysticism. And, of course, in ways and means that cannot begin to be enumerated, women such as St. Elizabeth of Hungary, Elizabeth Ann Seton, and Mother Teresa of Calcutta have done much for the church's missionary, educational, evangelical, medicinal, and charitable apostolates of charity.

God did not refrain from utilizing women in such pivotal ways and means to ensure that the saving designs of salvation were mediated to humanity. God employed women in the unsurpassable act of God communicating God's love to humanity through the Christ Event. Women accompanied and provided for Jesus and his ministry and were counted among his apostles. Women established and led early Christian communities.

Women made prolific contributions to the theological and mystical traditions of the church. Women ensured the perennial perpetuation of the church's apostolates. Women were entrusted with the saving mysteries central to the Christian faith. Given and in light of this, the Catholic Church, echoing the apostle Paul in his letter to the Galatians (3:28), now sees that with God there is neither male nor female and henceforth the church entrusts the saving mysteries of the faith—the sacraments—and the leadership of ecclesial communities to women as well as men.

ONE CAN ALMOST IMAGINE what the future magisterial document will sound like when the Roman Catholic Church comes to ordain women, entrusting them to serve as mediators of God's grace acting in the person of Jesus on behalf of the church while presiding over the sacraments and serving as leaders within the church. Theology ought not denigrate common sense. If Scripture attests to God trusting women with the central mysteries of the Christian faith—assent to the Incarnation, presence at the death of Jesus, and witness and proclaimer of Jesus' resurrection—then who are we not to entrust women with the saving mysteries of the faith we experience as the sacraments? No human theological articulations or ecclesial disciplines trump the revealed actions of God.

I must confess that as I was discerning this book I was struck by a profound incredulity. I cannot understand why there is not more outrage regarding the maltreatment of women within the Christian churches. Sadly, such maltreatment of women is all too common throughout the majority of the world's religions. As the imagined beginning of a potential future magisterial document on women in the Catholic Church above indicates, salvation history is chock full of women serving as mediators of God's saving wisdom and designs. There is a plethora of examples of women establishing and leading faith communities and serving as apostles and disciples of Jesus. Women accompanied Jesus, provided for the Christian movement, and perpetuated the ministerial apostolates of the church throughout the centuries. Women were the primary figures entrusted with the saving mysteries which are the Christ Event at the heart of Christianity (Jesus' birth, death, and resurrection).[1] Again, if women were chosen by God for such roles and tasks, then who are we to impede them from them now? Can one honestly fathom God creating an ecclesial and sacramental system that excludes one half of the human population from authentic participation on par and with the same integrity afforded the other half? I have been blessed

1. John Paul II, *Mulieris Dignitatem*, secs. 13–17, 27.

to have three sons. If I imagine that I may have had daughters, and consider those who do, I am pained to think of what many Christian churches, including my own Catholic Church, are communicating to them.

As I shared in the introduction, over the span of my thirty years of teaching in Catholic colleges/universities, the majority of my students majoring in theology have been women. It is also my experience that it is women, like these, who have become the most theologically educated and ministerially active in the contemporary American church. I have come to dub these faithful women who have blessed my teaching career the *anawim*. In scripture the *anawim* are depicted as the faithful remnant through whom God perpetuates God's saving designs for humanity within their respective faith communities. My *anawim* do the same. They now serve as teachers, youth ministers, directors of religious education, hospital chaplains, missionaries, and counselors in Catholic parishes and institutions. Some of these women believe that they have been called by God for ordained ministry in the Catholic Church. It is for them that I hope that the imagined future magisterial statement might come to be. It is them who I have in mind as I compose this chapter. A dear friend of mine gifted with the charisms of tongues, healing, and a call to ordination eventually left the Catholic Church and is seeking ordination in the Episcopal Church. She did so because God called her to ordination, and if the Catholic Church ordained women she would still be Catholic. I do not want these young graduates who are also called to pastoral leadership to have leaving the church as their only option to answer the call. When is the time for women such as these not to have to choose between fidelity to God's call and remaining Catholic? When is the time for women such as these to have ordained ministries within the Catholic Church? When? Now.

CALL VS. ORDINATION

In theology precision of language (and terms) as well as intellectual integrity are important. Current Catholic teachings which underpin the church's exclusion of women from sacramental and leadership roles in the church sometimes lack the aforesaid. Consistent in magisterial teachings regarding the exclusion of women from ordination and positions of ecclesial authority is a pervasive distortion of scripture and a posited example alleged to have been established by Jesus. In a non-critical manner, devoid of credible scriptural support, the magisterium equates the call of the twelve disciples (all men) with ordination to the priesthood.[2] This is in despite of the fact that nowhere in scripture are the twelve ordained, or called priests, or depicted as confecting the Eucharist. Here is why precision in language and terms matter.

The magisterium makes the jump from "call" to "ordination" and equates the two in spite of the aforesaid lack of scriptural warrant to do so. Hence language and terminology are distorted and the eventuating stance of prohibition against women being ordained is devoid of intellectual integrity. If one is to employ the notion of call as being equal to ordination, who can rightfully claim with any legitimacy that no woman has ever received a call to priesthood from God?[3] Other Christian traditions are chock full of female priests. Among the students and friends whom I referred to in the introduction and above, I know a number of Catholic women who have received such a call and who suffer greatly because of the Catholic Church's disciplines and praxis. These disciplines and praxis impede them from responding as they have discerned what God wills for them. To suggest that they are mistaken and/or are confused by the nature of the call, for any possible call from God for them could only be to some other ecclesial ministry or service other than ordination, leadership or authority, is simply not compelling. It is patronizing. Ecclesial marginalization, subordination, and exclusion of women from ecclesial sacramental and leadership roles ought not be attempted to be justified by a distorted reading of scripture with an accompanying inaccurate equation of call to ordination. Complicating matters further is a problematic presumption regarding the mind and will of Jesus proffered by magisterial teachings.

THE MIND AND WILL OF JESUS?

In addition to the unsubstantiated call of the twelve being equal to ordination unto the priesthood, magisterial teachings which exclude women from ecclesial sacramental and leadership roles also consistently employ a claim that the aforesaid call of the twelve illuminates the mind and will of Jesus regarding ecclesial leadership and the sacramental economy of the church.[4]

---

2. John Paul II, *Ordinatio Sacerdotalis, Mulieris Dignitatem*, sec. 26; Congregation Doctrine of Faith, *Inter Insigniores*, secs. 1–2.

3. Congregation Doctrine for Faith, *Inter Insigniores*, sec. 6.

4. John Paul II, *Ordinatio Sacerdotalis*, and *Mulieris Dignitatem*, sec. 26; Congregation Doctrine of Faith, *Inter Insigniores*, sec. 4.

The Congregation for the Doctrine of Faith, in *Inter Insigniores*, waffles in terms of consideration of historical and cultural influences upon Jesus and the apostles when it denies that the attitudes of Jesus and the apostles can be explained by the influence of their milieu and their times when it comes to the ordination of women, while simultaneously and inconsistently positing that other ordinances (women covering their heads and refraining from speaking in ecclesial assemblies) determined by the aforesaid were "probably inspired by the customs of the period."[5] While at times acknowledging that prejudices unfavorable to women have influenced ecclesial history and writings, the Congregation rejects that such prejudices could have influenced the pastoral activities or spiritual directions of the Fathers of the church.[6] Likewise, Pope John Paul II, in *Mulieris Dignitatem*, asserted that in calling only men as apostles:

> Jesus acted in a completely free and sovereign manner . . . without conforming to the prevailing customs and to the traditions sanctioned by the legislation of the time. Consequently, the assumption that he called men to be apostles in order to conform with the widespread mentality of his times, does not at all correspond to Christ's way of acting.[7]

I believe such assertions fail to honor Jesus' incarnate human nature and faculties as came to be understood and defined in the early Christological councils of the fourth through seventh centuries. The composite teachings of the councils of Nicea, I Constantinople, Ephesus, Chalcedon, and III Constantinople come to constitute what Christians believe and maintain about the personhood and natures of Jesus.[8] There is only one Jesus. Jesus is co-eternal with God throughout all eternity through whom God created the universe. Jesus was also born of the Virgin Mary in time, assuming human nature. Jesus has only one personhood that never, ever changes—a divine one. The same person co-eternal with God from all eternity through whom all was created is the same person born of Mary in time assuming human nature. Prior to the Incarnation Jesus had not only a divine personhood but also a divine nature which was of the same divine nature and essence

5. Congregation Doctrine of Faith, *Inter Insigniores*, sec. 4.

6. Congregation Doctrine of Faith, *Inter Insigniores*, sec. 1.

7. John Paul II, *Mulieris Dignitatem*, sec. 26.

8. Neuner and Dupuis, *The Christian Faith*, 155–84; Kelly, *Early Christian Doctrines*, 233–400; Davis, *The First Seven Ecumenical Councils*, 325–787; Bellitto, *The General Councils*, 17–30; O'Collins, *Christology*, 153–249; Helminiak, *The Same Jesus*, 19f.

of God. Jesus was and is *homoousios*/consubstantial with God vis-à-vis the divine nature. Via the Incarnation Jesus assumes human nature. The same Jesus who was and is a divine person, who shared the same divine nature as God, assumed a human nature that was united to Jesus' personhood.

The mystery of the Hypostatic Union posits that in the single divine person of Jesus divine and human natures are united. One divine personhood, two natures, divine and human. The union of the natures is in the personhood of Jesus, not the natures themselves. In fact, the early councils assert that the two respective natures are never mixed or confused (united to one another), as well as never divided (separate from Jesus' single personhood). Rather, the two respective natures are united in the single divine personhood of Jesus. We can see clearly that precision in language and terminology regarding the personhood and natures of Jesus is crucially important in understanding the mystery of Jesus.

Within the study of Christology consideration of how the attributes of Jesus' respective natures, human and divine, were operative while Jesus was incarnate is known as the communication of idioms.[9] Since Jesus was only one person, a divine one, it could be suggested that the divine person utilized divine nature at times, human nature at other times, while incarnate. This would suggest that Jesus' divine nature was operative while he was incarnate in a manner that need not mix and confuse the two respective natures, divine and human, themselves. In what follows, I will suggest a legitimate understanding of how Jesus utilized, or refrained from utilizing, his respective natures, human and divine, while incarnate. In order to be the New Adam, to take on a complete and authentic human nature, and to redeem and save humanity by undoing what Adam did, Jesus, out of his *agapic* (unconditional) and *kenotic* (self-emptying) love for human beings and fidelity to the saving plans of God, refrained from utilizing his divine nature while incarnate. I believe that such an understanding honors the teachings of the early Christological councils and is faithful to traditional Christian soteriology. All acts of Jesus can be said to be divine for they were conducted by a divine person. This need not necessitate that his divine nature was operative while incarnate. Even miracles—which the apostles replicate—do not necessitate the operation of a divine nature.

In light of Christian soteriology (theology of salvation), the councils discussed above further posited that "what was not taken on was not saved." In other words, if there was an aspect of our human nature not assumed

---

9. Davis, *First Seven Ecumenical Councils*, 325–787, 176, 327.

by Jesus via the Incarnation, then that aspect of our humanity would not be redeemed and saved. To be savior of fallen human nature Jesus had to assume human nature in its entirety, especially a human mind and will, as the councils attest. It was human nature that fell. It was human nature that needed to be redeemed. For Jesus to be the New Adam, the new human being, and undo what Adam did (misused the human faculties of reason and will in a manner that distorted God's providential designs), Jesus must be fully and authentically human. Due to the misuse of reason and will human beings distort the truth and transgress God's providential designs and intentions for human conduct. At the heart of human sin is human misuse of these two faculties, rationality and volition. Jesus saves humanity for he takes on the fullness of human nature and utilizes a human mind and human will in complete accordance to the will of God. Thereby Jesus restores for humanity the created order intended by God. If one unites oneself in faith to Jesus, Jesus imputes his righteousness to us, rendering us adopted children justified by God.[10]

I articulate the above synopsis of Christian soteriology to accentuate that Christianity maintains that in order for Jesus to be savior of humanity he must assume an authentic and complete human nature. This includes a human mind and a human will. To compromise or inflate Jesus' sharing of human nature is to put Christian soteriology at risk. Or, stated differently, while considering Jesus' incarnate human nature one must hold that he utilized an authentic and complete human nature, including a human mind and will. Furthermore, his faculties of human nature were not mixed or confused with his divine nature. To save humanity, while incarnate Jesus utilized only his human nature. The divine nature remained united to Jesus' personhood but, out of Jesus' *kenotic* love for humanity and in obedience to God's providential design to save humanity via the Christ Event, while on earth Jesus utilized only a human nature. To suggest that Jesus' divine nature was operative while incarnate would make Jesus something other (more) than human.

Given the central soteriological importance of Jesus assuming an authentic and complete human nature while incarnate, including a human mind and will, it is problematic to make appeals to the mind or will of Jesus in order to underpin and legitimize ecclesial disciplines and practices presumed to be perennially and perpetually binding upon ecclesial

10. *Romans*

praxis.[11] This is because, in light of the consensus teachings of the early Christological councils outlined above, Jesus utilized a human mind and will while incarnate. As such, Jesus' human nature, including his human mind and will, would have been subject to the same possibilities as well as limitations of any other human being.

While incarnate Jesus' decisions and actions, informed by an authentic and complete human nature, would have been subject to those things that all human beings are subject to: culture, context, history, socio-political and economic realities, conditions, customs, norms, mores, education, etc. Jesus' determinations while incarnate and utilizing a human nature must be respected as such. Jesus' determinations while incarnate and utilizing a human nature, mind, and will would, therefore, be limited to the possibilities and limitations of his human nature. As such, to posit a determination made by Jesus while incarnate as perennially and perpetually binding is to do an injustice to his human nature, mind, and will. It is to suggest that somehow his divine nature overshadowed, turned off, or mixed and confused with his human nature, thereby rendering a determination made by something other than an authentic and complete human nature. To suggest such adulterates Jesus' authentic and complete human nature and thereby places Christian soteriology at risk.

Hence, ecclesial appeals to the mind and will of Jesus as presenting a perennially and perpetually binding example for all subsequent ecclesial history and praxis is problematic. Even if Jesus did only choose men among the twelve, such a choice would have been shaped, colored, and informed by the cultural, socio-political, economic, and religious conditions which prevailed at the time. Such a choice, then, would be limited, as are all human decisions. They would not be perennially and perpetually binding. To suggest otherwise, to suggest as the magisterium has, "that Christ's way of acting did not proceed from sociological or cultural motives peculiar to his time . . . in calling only men as his apostles, Christ acted . . . without conforming to the prevailing customs and to the traditions sanctioned by the legislation of the time,"[12] fails to honor Jesus' authentic and complete human nature while incarnate. It is also seemingly inconsistent with the consensus of the early Christological councils and Christian soteriology. As noted above, scripture records Jesus as having called the twelve, not ordaining them to the priesthood as ordination came to evolve over time.

11. John Paul II, *Ordinatio Sacerdotalis*, and *Mulieris Dignitatem*.
12. John Paul II, *Ordinatio Sacerdotalis*, sec. 2.

Regarding Jesus' knowledge while incarnate, utilizing a complete and authentic human nature, including a human mind and human will, it would seem that all we could say with certainty about Jesus' knowledge, without compromising or inflating Jesus' human nature, is that it would be limited to what he could have ascertained utilizing a human mind. Is it possible that Jesus' divine personhood informed his human mind? Perhaps. While incarnate was Jesus aware of his divine personhood? Perhaps. Such questions lie at the center of what is frequently referred to as debates regarding messianic consciousness in Christological studies.[13]

The extent of such influence and awareness, however, would be limited to what Jesus might have come to understand about his divine personhood while utilizing a human mind and human will. When you or I pray contemplatively and look deep within ourselves we are utilizing a human nature (human mind, will, and prayer life) and discover a human personhood. Jesus alone had the unique contemplative situation and opportunity of utilizing a human nature (human mind, will, and prayer life) and discovering within himself a divine personhood. This is what we can say with certitude. Anything else would be conjecture. Furthermore, if Jesus while incarnate, utilizing a human mind, will, and prayer life did, in fact, contemplatively discover his divine personhood, his understanding of such a discovery would have been limited to what his human mind could grasp. Given Jesus' divine personhood it can be said that Jesus acts were divine. However, this need not mean that Jesus' acts were conducted by employing divine nature.

SYMBOLIC EFFICACY AND METAPHORICAL INTELLIGIBILITY

Additional magisterial arguments underpinning the exclusion of women from ordination and ecclesial leadership are also problematic. At times it is suggested that women cannot be ordained because of requisite necessity of affinity which must exist between a symbol and its referent (that to which a symbol points and makes present).[14] The gist of the argument is that if the ordained is ontologically endowed with a character (indelible mark/seal

13. For consideration of the debate regarding messianic consciousness, see Brown, *Introduction to New Testament Christology*, 23–102; Helminiak, *The Same Jesus*, 195–224.

14. Pius XII, *Sacramentum Ordinis*, Congregation Doctrine of Faith, *Inter Insigniores*, secs. 4–5, John Paul II, *Mulieris Dignitatem*, secs. 25–26; Zagano, *Holy Saturday*, 40–44, 50–53.

upon one's soul) so as to enable them to serve as a mediating symbol acting in the person of Jesus, then the one being ordained must be a man. This is because, it is maintained, as a symbol the ordained must have an affinity to the referent, which is Jesus, who was male. In the words of the Congregation for the Doctrine of Faith, "When Christ's role in the Eucharist is to be expressed sacramentally, there would not be this natural resemblance which must exist between Christ and his minister if the role of Christ were not taken by a man . . ."[15]

Additionally, a significant metaphorical analogy to depict God's relationship with Israel and Christ's relationship to the church is biblically articulated in terms of God and Jesus as grooms vis-à-vis their respective brides, namely the covenanted people of Israel and the ecclesial community. Based upon this analogy, it is maintained that the one acting in the place of Jesus on behalf of the ecclesial community, whose presidency at the Eucharist perpetuates the saving mystery of God's redemptive covenant with humanity, must be a male:[16]

> . . . It must be admitted that, in actions which demand the character of ordination and in which the Christ, himself, the author of the Covenant, the Bridegroom, the Head of the Church, is represented exercising his ministry of salvation—which is in the highest degree the case of the Eucharist—his role . . . must be taken by a man.[17]

> As the Redeemer of the world, Christ is the Bridegroom of the Church. The Eucharist is the sacrament of our redemption. It is the sacrament of the Bridegroom and of the Bride. The Eucharist makes present and realizes anew in a sacramental manner the redemptive act of Christ.
>
> It is the Eucharist above all that expresses the redemptive act of Christ the Bridegroom towards the Church the Bride. This is clear and unambiguous when the sacramental ministry of the Eucharist, in which the priest acts *in persona Christi*, is performed by a man.[18]

Such assertions elevate a nuptial ecclesial metaphor and its image of spousal love between God and humanity, Jesus and the church, to an

---

15. Congregation Doctrine of Faith, *Inter Insigniores*, sec 5.

16. John Paul II, *Mulieris Dignitatem*, secs 23–26.

17. Congregation Doctrine of Faith, *Inter Insigniores*, sec. 5.

18. John Paul II, *Mulieris Dignitatem*, sec. 26.

absolutist status in spite of the fact that scripture affords us other meta-phorical analogies which bespeak of the relationship between God and human beings. These include espousing God as a loving, caring, and nursing mother,[19] as well as a protective hen and widow seeking out a lost coin.[20] Obviously, when it comes to analogous depictions and human comprehension of the relationship which exists between God and humanity, and Jesus and the church, no single metaphor can possibly exhaust or convey the mysteries of said relationships. Therefore, no one metaphor ought to be so absolutized so as to preclude others.

There is merit in suggesting that symbolic efficacy requires that there be an affinity and intelligibility between symbols and analogous metaphors and their referents. However, the problem lies with suggesting maleness as an exclusive and exhaustive requisite for there to be an affinity between the one ordained to act in the person of Jesus and convey God's covenantal love for human beings. Maleness alone does not ensure affinity to Jesus, nor analogously exhaust the love of God. Indeed, what constitutes a greater affinity to Jesus and God, maleness or an example of *hesed* (covenental), *agapic* (unconditional), and *kenotic* (self-sacrificial) love? Such as those I discuss above and in the introduction, women, as well as men, are capable of being efficacious symbols acting in the person of Jesus and communicating the love of God. This is so if their witness is one imbued with an affinity to Jesus and the love of God. To suggest that a pedophile male priest and/or a bishop culpable of covering up ecclesial scandal can be a more efficacious symbol of Jesus or more effectively communicate the love of God than Mother Teresa of Calcutta because of their maleness is not compelling. It is absurd.

HISTORICAL ORDINATION OF WOMEN

Again, precision of language and intellectual honesty matter in theology. It is simply not true to suggest that women were never ordained by the church. While still a united church in the first millennium of the Common Era, women were in fact ordained. There is a plethora of historical records which reveal that women were ordained to the diaconate and that

---

19. Isa 49:14–15, 66:13, Ps 131:2–3; John Paul II, *Mulieris Dignitatem*, sec. 8.
20. Matt 23:37; Luke 13:34; 15:8–10.

the leaders of women religious communities, abbesses, were ordained.[21] Women may not have been ordained to the presbyterate, but they were clearly ordained to the diaconate and in their roles as superiors of female religious communities. Precision of language and intellectual honesty are warranted. Women were and have been ordained.

The historical fact of women serving in apostolic and ministerial roles within the early Christian church finds its roots and inspiration in scripture. Scripture bespeaks of women as apostolic evangelizers counted among Jesus' apostles who were members of early Christian missionary efforts of evangelization. In Romans, Paul speaks of Phoebe as the deaconess of Cenchrea (Rom. 16:1–2). It should be noted that Paul is referring Phoebe to the fledgling Christian community in Rome, beseeching the community there to receive Phoebe as an authority. I Timothy 3:8–11 describes women deacons vis-à-vis male deacons as recognized servants within the ecclesial community marked by being respectable, trustworthy, reliable, sober, and tempered in speech. Luke 8:1–3 describes Jesus as making his way through towns and villages preaching and proclaiming the Good News of the kingdom of God accompanied by women who had experienced cures at the hands of Jesus, as well as by Mary Magdalene, Joanna, Susanna, and others who provided for Jesus and the twelve out of their own resources. Additionally, Luke seemingly includes women among the mission of seventy-two apostles sent out by Jesus to proclaim the kingdom of God and to spread the peace which Jesus has to offer.[22]

St. Clement of Alexandria (c. 150–215 CE) testifies to women deacons and maintains that women were chosen by the apostles to serve as co-ministers in carrying out their pastoral duties just as Paul had prescribed.[23] Commenting on the passage in Romans which speaks of Phoebe as deaconess, Origen (c. 184–253 CE) asserted that the text taught with the authority of Paul that women were instituted deacons in the church.[24] The liturgical treatise of the first half of the third century, the *Didascalia Apostolorum*, marks the initial time that deaconesses appear in an ecclesial document. It presents deaconesses in a typological fashion as the anti-types of the Holy Spirit chosen by the bishop for works of charity and service of

---

21. International Theological Commission, *Diakonia Christ to Apostles* 14; Zagano, *Holy Saturday*, 107–111; Wijngaards, *Women Deacons*, 85–90.

22. Luke 10:1–12.

23. Wijngaards, *Women Deacons*, 15.

24. Origen, *Commentary on Romans*, 89; Wijngaards, *Women Deacons*, 15.

women such as baptismal anointing, catechetical instruction, and visitation to the sick.[25] The Councils of Nicea (325 CE) and Chalcedon (451 CE) both have Canons regarding the ordination of women to the diaconate.[26] In light of this historical evidence, the International Theological Commission's 2002 document, *From the Diakonia of Christ to the Diakonia of the Apostles*, states matter-of-factly that "from the end of the third century onwards, in certain regions of the church (and not all of them), a specific ecclesial ministry is attested to on the part of women called deaconesses."[27]

Subsequent ecclesial history illuminates that within the Christian tradition, in time, deaconesses became members of a distinct clerical class designated as such via episcopal imposition of hands and *epiclesis*.[28] As noted above, from the fourth century on, women in charge of female monastic communities, abbesses, were ordained and also commonly referred to as deaconesses, a practice confirmed by Canon 15 of Chalcedon (451).[29] In the East, episcopal imposition of hands upon deaconesses who served as superiors to monasteries of women continued through the eighth century whereby deaconesses were ordained in the ecclesial sanctuary within the context of a Eucharistic liturgy, just as were male deacons.[30] Likewise, the presence of deaconesses in Rome is attested to through the end of the eighth century.[31]

Hence, to be precise and intellectually honest, women were ordained within the history of the church. Women were thereby made members of the clergy via episcopal imposition of hands and *epiclesis*. Although their ministries may have been an extension of the bishops' and directed mainly toward fellow women due to sensitivities of propriety, or leadership of female monasteries (as the International Theological Commission's *From the Diakonia of Christ to the Diakonia of the Apostles* accentuates), their

25. International Theological Commission, *Diakonia Christ to Apostles*, 12–13; Vagaggini, *Ordination of Women to Diaconate*, 10–18; 29–30.

26. International Theological Commission, *Diakonia Christ to Apostles*, 14; Zagano, *Holy Saturday*, 74; Vagaggini, *Ordination of Women to Diaconate*, 20.

27. International Theological Commission, *Diakonia Christ to Apostles*, 12.

28. International Theological Commission, *Diakonia Christ to Apostles*, 13–14; Wijngaards, *Women Deacons*, 34–49; 104–5.

29. International Theological Commission, *Diakonia Christ to Apostles*, 13–14; Wijngaards, *Women Deacons*, 84–90.

30. Vagaggini, *Ordination of Women to Diaconate*, 45–56; Wijngaards, *Women Deacons*, 24–25; 31–49; 100–107.

31. International Theological Commission, *Diakonia Christ to Apostles*, 19.

ordination was no different from male deacons and their participation in clerical orders no different either. Given these apostolic and historical precedents, there is no legitimacy to suggest that women were never ordained. Nor are there any compelling reasons not to consider ordaining women again now if the pastoral needs of the faithful necessitate such and if the Spirit is asking the church to do so. In light of this historical record, my friend discussed above ought not to have had to choose between honoring God's call to ordination and remaining Catholic.

Granted, the historical evidence outlined above highlights the ordination of women deaconesses and abbesses, not female ordination unto the priesthood. However, given the jump from call of the twelve to ordination and consideration of sacramental symbolic and ecclesial metaphorical efficacy and affinity outlined above, if the pastoral needs of the church warranted ordaining women to the priesthood, and the Holy Spirit inspired such, there is no compelling reason to not ordain women to the priesthood as well.

Ongoing Dialogue and Meaningful Advances

Simply asserting that "the non-admission of women to priestly ordination cannot mean that women are of lesser dignity, nor can it be construed as discrimination against them,"[32] as magisterial teachings do, quite simply rings shallow. How does such a stance not ring as an affront to the dignity of women and discrimination against them? Likewise, to simply try to will away contemporary consideration of restoring female ordination by declaring that the church's position of excluding women from ordination must be "definitively held," as *Ordinatio Sacerdotalis* asserts,[33] is intellectually offensive and repugnant, and pastorally irresponsible. One cannot simply wish away something that the Spirit is moving among people. Nor does such a stance reflect the best of Catholic theology which is open to the exchange of ideas. The great Dominican doctor of the church, St. Thomas Aquinas, dubbed the perennial theologian of the church, employing Scholastic theological methodology, cites, in his *magnus opus*, the *Summa Theologiae*, those who object to his positions, entertains them, and responds to them. He does not ignore them nor wish them away. Likewise, Pope John Paul II, in *Fides et Ratio*, assured that faith need not fear reason, rather the two

32. John Paul II, *Ordinatio Sacerdotalis*, sec. 3.
33. John Paul II, *Ordinatio Sacerdotalis*, sec. 4.

work together to edify and enrich human understanding. The best of the Catholic intellectual tradition does not wish away dialogue and discussion, nor fear opposing points of view. Nothing is to be gained intellectually or pastorally by trying to do so.

Whatever position one might hold regarding the ordination of women and their inclusion within positions of ecclesial authority and the church's sacramental economy, I think we can all agree that the language that the church employs to exclude women from ordination and positions of ecclesial authority ought not be condescending and patronizing. Nor should it perpetuate a historical caricature of women which tends to reduce women to maternal or passive characterizations. Likewise, it should not juxtapose women to Mary in a manner which suggests that proper imitation of her requires acceptance of one's role with an accompanying deference to male and heavenly authorities.[34] Although of great value, maternity does not exhaust the gifts of women, and Mary was no shrinking violet. Indeed, Mary is at the center of the salvific event, of Jesus' messianic service, and is *theotokos*.[35] Characterizations of women which perpetuate disadvantages to women and male domination over them is a perpetuation of sin which disturbs the equal dignity that women and men share as the image and likeness of God.[36]

The Vatican's 2004 *Letter to the Bishops of the Catholic Church on the Collaboration of Men and Women in the Church and in the World* suggests that, "Woman, in her deepest and original being, exists 'for the other.'"[37] The women whom I know who are called to ordained ministry and positions of ecclesial authority wish precisely to be for others. Why does the church unjustly circumscribe how they are able to be so? If women inherently have a "capacity for the other" as the same document maintains,[38] what could more effectively convey God's love for humanity than to serve as an ordained minister? What could have a greater affinity to the example of Jesus and therefore be a more intelligible or efficacious symbol of God and Jesus than that? Deeming that "the reservation of priestly ordination

---

34. John Paul II, *Mulieris Dignitatem*, secs. 17–19.

35. John Paul II, *Mulieris Dignitatem*, secs. 3–5.

36. John Paul II, *Mulieris Dignitatem*, sec. 10.

37. Congregation Doctrine of Faith, *Letter to Bishops on Collaboration of Men and Women*, 6.

38. Congregation Doctrine of Faith, *Letter to Bishops on Collaboration of Men and Women*, 13.

solely to men does not hamper in any way women's access to the heart of the Christian life," as the Vatican's 2004 *Letter on Collaboration* does,[39] is simply not compelling. If the church is going to champion human dignity, condemn discrimination, and hold other entities to ensuring that women are present within the world of work and societal organizations at the levels of responsibility over policies and solutions to problems,[40]ought the church not practice and exemplify that which it preaches? Failure to do so compromises the church's prophetic voice and Catholic social teaching, and renders the church's challenge to other entities duplicitous and disingenuous.

The United States Conference of Catholic Bishops seemingly concurs when the bishops call for the active and responsible presence of women in the church's leadership being realized in practice in their pastoral letter, *From Words to Deeds*.[41] The American bishops go on to suggest that the movement for greater roles for women in ecclesial ministry and leadership is a movement inspired by the Holy Spirit to ensure the church's missionary effectiveness and so that the church as a community itself is a credible and effective sign to the world.[42] The bishops also recognize the need for the church to continually reform and renew its structures and practices to be a more effective instrument. They note that such efforts entail the engagement of the gifts of all its members while simultaneously acknowledging that, "Too often women's gifts have gone unnoticed and undervalued . . . while their dignity has often been unacknowledged and their prerogatives misrepresented . . . often relegated to the margins . . . and even reduced to servitude . . . stereotyped into roles that do not allow them to exercise all their gifts."[43] The bishops even go on to suggest that they see how "the Holy Spirit grants new gifts in response to changing historical circumstances" while calling for the gifts of women in the areas of "prayer, worship, leadership, teaching and organization," suggesting that they could enrich the church.[44]

---

39. Congregation Doctrine of Faith, *Letter to Bishops on Collaboration of Men and Women*, 16.

40. Congregation Doctrine of Faith, *Letter to Bishops on Collaboration of Men and Women*, 13.

41. US Catholic Bishops, *Words to Deeds*, 2.

42. US Catholic Bishops, *Words to Deeds*, 3–4.

43. US Catholic Bishops, *Words to Deeds*, 5, 10.

44. US Catholic Bishops, *Words to Deeds*, 5.

However, alas, the pastoral suggestions, goals, and calls to action that the bishops proffer do not existentially go beyond echoing sentiments regarding the expanded number of "educated, talented and experienced women changing the face of the church, calls to appoint women to positions which entail substantive responsibility and influence whereby women can exercise leadership in the church and be true collaborators in church decision-making processes."[45] Pacifying repetition of tried (and tired) ecclesial discourse accompanied by scant token references to particular isolated diocesan initiatives ultimately only serves to perpetuate the same old same old condescending and patronizing consideration of women in the church. Authentic empowerment of women is what is needed. True and meaningful reform of institutional structures, vehicles, and mechanisms is what is needed. Praxis, not mere sentiment, is needed. Affording women the same and full opportunities within the church enjoyed by men is what is needed—sacramentally and authoritatively. It is time for the bishops to stop talking about the dignity of women and time to honor it in praxis. It is time for the bishops to stop talking about institutional ecclesial reform and to reform the church and change its structures, vehicles, and mechanisms. When? Now.

A Missed Opportunity

As I was preparing to write this book there was within the Catholic Church a possibility that some significant headway might be made for the cause of women's ordination, sacramental presidency, and share in ecclesial authority. The Amazonian bishops had recently conducted a synod during which they considered the pastoral crises facing a number of their faithful and potential pastoral solutions which might help to address the pastoral needs of their people. The synod noted that many Amazonian communities go for a year or more without the Eucharist and other sacraments because of a serious shortage of priests.[46] One of the things that the bishops considered was expanding the roles of women within the sacramental and leadership roles of the church in the Amazon. On February 2, 2020, Pope Francis issued his post-synodal exhortation, *Querida Amazonia*, in which he closed any small opening of a window for the cause of women in the Amazonian church

---

45. US Catholic Bishops, *Words to Deeds*, 7, 9.

46. Hansen, "Top Five Takeaways from the Amazon Synod," Schillebeeckx, *Church Human Face.*

which might have cracked open. The document does speak at length about the need for ecclesial inculturation (even at the ministerial and organizational levels) and openness to the Spirit so as to discover new ways to meet the pastoral needs of the faithful.[47] However, it ultimately fails to honor how women might be empowered in sacramental and leadership roles in new substantive and authoritative ways. Sadly, in spite of the pope's calls that the "feminine genius" and women decision making and authoritative participation in the structures and life of the church be more vitally incorporated into ecclesial life that have marked his papacy,[48] the Amazonian document lapses back into conventional hierarchical patronizing, subordination, and condescension of women.

The pope has the audacity to voice suggestions that ordaining women would actually reduce their import within the church, suggesting that to ordain women would be to narrow their roles within the church by clericalizing them. It is suggested that doing so would diminish their value and render their contributions less effective.[49] He goes on to differentiate women's roles within the church by juxtaposing their ecclesial contributions to that of Mary, as opposed to the contributions of men which are juxtaposed to Jesus. He suggests that each set of contributions are proper to each sex, respectively corresponding to two different aspects of Jesus' revealed love.[50] The pope further suggests that to ordain women would be paramount to reducing their contributions to one of understanding them solely in terms of functionality, thereby reducing and limiting them.[51] Ironically, as will be explored in the next chapter which considers homosexuality, the church does not have a problem with reducing the complexus of human sexuality to functionality.

Such propositions are simply not compelling, nor credible, nor do they honor the very thing the pope pines for, namely an ecclesial openness to the emergence of forms of service and charisms of women to respond to specific needs of the people of the Amazon region at this moment in

47. Francis, *Querida Amazonia*, secs. 66–9, 85.

48. For example, Francis has appointmented a woman to a managerial position within the Vatican Secretariat of State and has convened a commission to study the matter of women deacons; Francis, *Christus Vivit*, sec. 42; Francis, *Evangelii Gaudium*, sec. 103.

49. Francis, *Querida Amazonia*, sec. 100.

50. Francis, *Querida Amazonia*, sec. 101.

51. Francis, *Querida Amazonia*, sec. 101.

history.[52] If the church is not to be "a static museum piece, but the root of a constantly growing tree, if the faith must become flesh in the culture of those who receive it, and if the Holy Spirit adorns the church, showing her new aspects of revelation . . . allowing and encouraging the inexhaustible riches of the gospel to be preached in categories proper to each culture, creating a new synthesis with that particular culture,"[53] as the pope suggests, then why not allow the church to grow? Why not allow the church to take flesh in new pneumatically inspired adornments which would render the gospel more meaningful, relevant, and viable to various respective cultures and better meet the pastoral needs of various peoples? Although stating that "what is needed is courageous openness to the novelty of the Spirit,"[54] as the pope does, such courage evidently falls short vis-à-vis pneumatic correctives regarding the ordination and authoritative empowerment of women. When it comes to the issue of women in the church, it seems as if the male hierarchy remains frightened, hiding locked in an attic still awaiting the Spirit and the courage the Spirit will provide to go forth to make the gospel available to all.

CONCLUSION

As noted above, I have had a number of female Catholic students and friends over the years who have expressed their call to ordination and leadership in the Catholic Church. I have witnessed their pain and frustration firsthand as they have been impeded by the disciplines and practices of their church. I have also had the privilege of personally having and knowing ordained female pastors who serve the Evangelical Lutheran Church of America. They do so as well as the male priests I have known who serve the Catholic churches to which I have also belonged over the same course of time. Women can and do preside over the Eucharist. Women can and do lead churches. Women can and do exercise ecclesial governance. And women should. Indeed, at the recitation of the words of institution during Eucharistic celebrations, "This is my body, given for you," I am always moved more powerfully when it is a woman presider articulating them. I am drawn back to when my wife was pregnant and subsequently breastfeeding our newborn sons. This was a time when, indeed, it was clear that

52. Francis, *Querida Amazonia*, sec. 102.

53. Francis, *Querida Amazonia*, sec. 66, 68.

54. Francis, *Querida Amazonia*, sec. 69.

her life was given to my sons so that they may have life in return. As much as I love my boys, my body could not gestate them nor afford them milk, nourishment, and sustenance from my breast so that I could say that this is my body, given for you, so that you may have life in return. To suggest that women are not capable of acting in the person of Jesus on behalf of the church, that they are not capable of being an effective symbol able to render the covenantal love of God and the referent of Jesus present, that they are deficient in terms of affinity to Jesus, is just wrong. I share the sentiment of Rachel Held Evans:

> On the days and nights I believe this story that we call Christianity, I cannot entirely make sense of the storyline: God trusted God's very self, totally and completely and in full bodily form, to the care of a woman. God needed women for survival. Before Jesus fed us with the bread and the wine, the body and the blood, Jesus himself needed to be fed, by a woman. He needed a woman to say: "This is my body, given for you."[55]

Those who know my wife would attest and concur with what I am about to write. Suzy is one of those rare individuals marked by an inexplicable joy that comes from Jesus' love dwelling in her. She radiates joy, love, and Jesus. Although she has never discerned the call to ordination, and absolutely loves being an elementary school librarian, it is simply unacceptable to entertain that an ecclesial tradition might impede and exclude her from ordained ministry if she were so called. Along with common sense, there is no substitute in theology for lived experience.

> The hour is coming, in fact has come, when the vocation of women is being acknowledged in its fullness, the hour in which women acquire in the world (and the church), an effect and a power never hitherto achieved . . . it is evident that women are meant to form part of the living and working structure of Christianity in so prominent a manner that perhaps not all their potential have yet been made clear.[56]

My sons and I, the majority of my students, and many others are no longer willing to tolerate the maltreatment of women within the church. We are no longer willing to see them impeded and excluded from sacramental presidency and positions of ecclesial authority and authentic decision

---

55. Evans, *Wholehearted Faith*, 4–5.
56. John Paul II, *Mulieris Dignitatem*, sec. 1.

making. We are outraged. When is the hour for women's ordination, empowerment, and expanded roles within ecclesial sacramental ministry and leadership? When? Now.

2

Homosexuality

IN THE INTRODUCTION I spoke of the emotional unsettledness I experienced as I worked on this book. With none of the topics addressed was this more true than with the focus of this chapter. I know many gay persons who suffer as a result of the Catholic Church's teachings regarding homosexuality and who, in light of these teachings, feel forced to live in fear as they work in various ministerial and educational apostolates of the church. They are gripped with the concern that they will be found out and subsequently forced out of their vocations and employment.[1] Over the years I have had a significant number of gay students. My wife, sons, and I have a number of gay friends. And it is becoming obvious that homosexuality touches an increasingly growing number of Catholic families. They often feel that the church is not welcoming to their gay loved ones, let alone that its actions honor the consistently-heralded message that all people are created in the image and likeness of God and thus possess an innate human dignity that must be acknowledged and respected.[2] Indeed, even as I was writing this book I learned that the weekly Sunday mass for the LGBTQ+ community of our diocese which had been held at a local Franciscan retreat center for more than 30 years had been repressed, and the that diocese of Milwaukee, Wisconsin, issued pastoral directives denying LGBTQ+ persons the sacraments.[3]

1. Gibson, "Miami Archbishop Warns Employees."

2. US Catholic Bishops, *Ministry Persons with Homosexual Inclination*, 2; *Catechism*, sec. 1700.

3. LGBTQ Catholics of Tampa Bay, "New Announcement;" Fraga, B. "Marquette Diocese's LGBTQ Restrictions Blasted."

Certain experiences over the course of my professional career particularly stand out to me regarding this issue. A priest friend who was a tenured colleague, who is gay, left the Catholic priesthood. He offered to leave the college at which we were employed for four years so that none of the current students would be scandalized by his decision. It was his hope that he could then return to his teaching position at the college. Instead, the college dismissed him immediately and indefinitely. Former students of mine who are gay serve in various diocesan apostolates and parish-based ministries and feel forced to live lives of secrecy and fear that their employment would be terminated if discovered. Students who have sought spiritual direction have confided in me that they have gay siblings and, as a result, find it difficult to balance their commitments to church teaching with the love that they have for their family members. Deacons and deacon candidates who I teach, in certain dioceses, are forbidden to attend wedding ceremonies of gay family members.

During my time of diocesan service I had to ask a donor to rescind his gift to one of our Catholic schools. He made a donation to the school in memory of his gay partner who had served the school for some thirty years. The concern was that the very thing that he was hoping to achieve via his gift—to memorialize his partner and support the school—would be undermined by certain elements within the church if it came to light that his partner was gay. What torturously painful situations for all of these persons to find themselves in.

In light of the breadth and depth of pain experienced by the plethora of people who I know that have been wounded by the church's teachings, attitudes, and disposition vis-à-vis homosexuality I felt moved by the Spirit to include consideration of homosexuality in this work. Additionally, whereas each of the focal topics of all of the other chapters contained in this book have some space within the tradition for debate and dialogue, the Catholic Church's teachings regarding homosexual genital physical expression (homosexual acts) are consistently unambiguous, thereby making engagement with this issue particularly challenging. The *Catechism of the Catholic Church* asserts:

> Basing itself on Sacred Scripture, which presents homosexual acts as acts of grave depravity, tradition has always declared that homosexual acts are intrinsically disordered. They are contrary to the natural law. They close the sexual act to the gift of life. They do

not proceed from a genuine affective and sexual complementarity. Under no circumstances can they be approved.[4]

This teaching leaves celibacy as the only option for homosexuals who are called to chastity, self-mastery, disinterested friendship, prayer, and grace as they strive for what is deemed Christian perfection.[5]

Homosexual Orientation vs. Homosexual Acts

Catholic moral theology has evolved in recent decades in its differentiation between the homosexual orientation and homosexual acts. The tradition has come to deem the orientation as morally neutral since the homosexual condition (orientation) is not chosen,[6] while continuing to condemn all homosexual acts. I imagine that such a distinction is little comfort to LG-BTQ+ persons for it is a distinction which presumes that acts can be morally assessed and evaluated independent and apart from human beings who act. Distinctions between acts and persons are false distinctions for there are no acts which are not conducted by persons. Although the distinction might stem from a sense of pastoral humility and care which, according to the Catechism, acknowledges that "the psychological genesis of homosexuality remains largely unexplained in spite of the fact that homosexuality has taken a great variety of forms through the centuries and in different cultures,"[7] the distinction ultimately fails pastorally because it is a false distinction. In condemning homosexual acts, LGBTQ+ persons are being condemned for there are no acts which are not conducted by persons. Reducing moral assessment to acts alone reduces the human person to a singular aspect of the complexus of what constitutes the human being. Doing so fails to take into consideration the whole person and other aspects which

4. *Catechism*, sec. 2357; US Catholic Bishops, *Ministry Persons with Homosexual Inclination*, 4.

5. *Catechism*, sec. 2359; Congregation Doctrine of Faith, *Letter on Pastoral Care of Homosexual Persons*, sec. 12.

6. *Catechism*, sec. 2358, US Catholic Bishops, *Ministry Persons with Homosexual Inclination*, 5, US Catholic Bishops, *Always Our Children*; Congregation Doctrine of Faith, *Letter on Pastoral Care of Homosexual Persons*, sec. 3.

7. *Catechism*, sec. 2357; Also note that in my research I found that there are far ranging opinions within the fields of biological, psychological, and social sciences when it comes to homosexuality and the role that genetics, hormones, brain anatomy/structure, and abuse may or may not play in homosexuality.

bear upon moral discernment such as intention (freedom and volition), circumstances (space and power), consequences, and relationality.

Ecclesial Inconsistency vis-à-vis Pastoral Language and Care for LGBTQ+ Persons

Further potential positive pastoral intentions are compromised by the Catholic Church's calls for homosexuals to be accepted with "respect, compassion and sensitivity . . . and insisting that every sign of unjust discrimination in their regard should be avoided,"[8] while the church fails to practice what it teaches. It does so by continuing to utilize language which speaks of homosexuals in terms of "depravity, intrinsically disordered, contrary to natural law," closed to the gift of life, disingenuous affective and sexual expression, self-indulgent, and contrary to the divine plan.[9] Such language is not respectful, compassionate, or sensitive. Additionally, in spite of decrying discrimination against homosexuals, the Catholic Church retains the right for itself to deny roles of service to homosexuals, to forbid homosexuals from public self-disclosure in the context of parish life, and offers no support of same sex civil unions and/or marriages, nor the adoption of children by same sex couples.[10] Furthermore, the church frequently discourages pastoral programs which include organizations in which homosexual persons associate with each other and calls for the withdrawal of any support given to organizations which may dissent from church teaching on homosexuality.[11] By not honoring the very thing it teaches, non-discrimination, the church's teaching is undermined by its own lack of example. Its teaching is rendered duplicitous and hypocritical. As the United States Conference of Catholic Bishops voiced in their 1987 Pastoral Letter, *Always Our Children*, "it is not sufficient to only avoid unjust discrimination, homosexual

---

8. *Catechism*, sec. 2358, Congregation Doctrine of Faith, *Letter Pastoral Care of Homosexual Persons*, sec. 10; US Catholic Bishops, *Always Our Children*.

9. US Catholic Bishops, *Ministry Persons with Homosexual Inclination*, 4; Congregation Doctrine of Faith, *Letter on Care of Homosexual Persons*, sec. 7.

10. US Catholic Bishops, *Ministry Persons with Homosexual Inclination*, 17, 20–21; US Bishops, *Always Our Children*.

11. Congregation Doctrine of Faith, *Letter Pastoral Care of Homosexual Persons*, secs. 15, 17; It should be noted that this discouraging of pastoral programs for homosexual persons voiced by the congregation is inconsistent with the United States Conference of Catholic Bishops' challenge to Christian communities to offer homosexuals pastoral care as voiced in their 1987 Pastoral Letter, *Always Our Children*.

persons must be accepted with respect, compassion and sensitivity."[12] Indeed, as Bishop Vincent Long Van Nguyen of Australia noted:

> We cannot talk about the integrity of creation, the universal and inclusive love of God, while at the same time colluding with the forces of oppression in the ill-treatment of . . . homosexual persons . . . It won't wash with young people, especially when we purport to treat gay people with love and compassion and yet define their sexuality as intrinsically disordered.[13]

HOMOSEXUALITY AND SCRIPTURE

Basing contemporary moral admonitions on appeals to scripture in a noncritical manner is intellectually problematic for a number of reasons.[14] This is particularly the case when considering aspects of human life which have come to be better understood over the centuries with the advent of new sciences. These new understandings shed new light on the complexity of human psychology and sociological development. The worldview and understandings of human sexuality held by the ancient Hebrews and followers of Jesus in the first century are not the same worldviews and understandings of Americans in the twenty-first century. Additionally, Catholic biblical scholarship embraces a historical-critical reading of scripture. Such an approach takes into consideration the dialectical nature of revelation whereby God takes the initiative to communicate to human beings but entrusts disclosures to human communities and authors in committing the message to writing.[15] Via this dialectical exchange revelation comes to be better understood over time as tradition progresses throughout the life of the church as the faith community grows in insights regarding the realities and words being passed on.[16] Guided by the Holy Spirit, the church advances in its understanding of truth.[17] However, this inspired dialecti-

---

12. US Catholic Bishops, *Always Our Children*.

13. Nguyen, *2016 Ann Clark Lecture*.

14. Gula, Richard M. S.S. "Scripture in Moral Theology," *Reason Informed by Faith*, 165–184; Freyne, "The Bible and Christian Morality," 9–32; Spohn, "What Are They Saying Scripture and Ethics," 313–321; Birch and Rasmussen, "Use of Bible Christian Ethics," 322–332.

15. *Dei Verbum*, secs. 1–7.

16. *Dei Verbum*, secs. 5, 8.

17. *Dei Verbum*, secs. 5, 7, 8, 11, 20.

cal process of improved understanding involves God speaking at different times and in various ways to human recipients who, according to the Second Vatican Council's *Dogmatic Constitution on Divine Revelation (Dei Verbum)*, "all the while employed in this task make full use of their powers and faculties."[18] As such, revelation entails God speaking to human beings in human fashion.

Therefore, when one reads scripture one must take into account what the human authors were intending to disclose and the literary forms of expression utilized. Account must also be made for the particular circumstances of time and culture in which they composed. Due attention must be made to the customary and characteristic patterns of perception, speech, narrative, and conventions which the people of the time followed in their dealings with one another which prevailed at the age of the writer.[19] Furthermore, the sacred writers of scripture wrote with an eye toward the particular situation of the various ecclesial communities to which they wrote.[20] In other words, utilizing scripture in a non-critical, proof-texting manner is a distortion of scripture and fails to honor the divine-human dialectic inherent in the process of revelation. Such a use of scripture is not compatible with the teachings regarding revelation and scripture promulgated in the Second Vatican Council's *Dogmatic Constitution on Divine Revelation (Dei Verbum)*.

If one takes seriously the dialectical nature of revelation and corresponding need to read scripture critically, as noted above, one must take into account the world view, culture, customs, conventions, historical time, and context, etc. which were operative at the time of composition. These factors, in turn, influenced and colored what was composed. Regretfully, magisterial teachings on homosexuality frequently fail to honor an approach to scripture as called for by *Dei Verbum*. Rather they tend towards non-critical proof-texting utilization of select biblical passages which tend to isolate biblical admonitions against homosexuality. They fail to adequately take into consideration the wider historical, cultural, theological, customary, and conventional understandings and contexts of the times in which the selected texts were composed. Not only is such a use of scripture inconsistent with the teachings of *Dei Verbum*, it also distorts the scriptural teaching itself. It constitutes a problematic proof-texting application

18. *Dei Verbum* secs. 4, 11.

19. *Dei Verbum*, sec. 12.

20. *Dei Verbum*, sec. 19.

to contemporary times devoid of both wider scriptural contextualization as well as ignorance of subsequent historical developments pertinent to human sexuality. These subsequent developments regarding sexuality have been illuminated with the advent of new discoveries regarding the psychosexual maturation and development of human beings which have come to light over the centuries with the development of modern social and behavioral sciences.

As illustrative, the United States Conference of Catholic Bishops' 2006 document, *Ministry to Persons with a Homosexual Inclination: Guidelines for Pastoral Care*, simply asserts in non-critical blanket fashion that:

> Whenever homosexual acts are mentioned in the Old Testament, it is clear that they are disapproved of, as contrary to the will of God. In the New Testament, St. Paul teaches that homosexual acts are not in keeping with our being created in God's image and so degrade and undermine our authentic dignity as human beings . . . homosexual practices can arise among people who erroneously worship the creature rather than the Creator . . . homosexual practices are among those things that are incompatible with the Christian life.[21]

Such sweeping condemnation of homosexuality is proffered devoid of any wider explication of the intentions or wider contexts of the scriptural authors. Nor do they convey any sense that our contemporary understandings of human sexuality differ significantly from that of the ancient Hebrews and first century followers of Jesus.

The Congregation for the Doctrine of the Faith's *Letter to the Bishops of the Catholic Church on the Pastoral Care of Homosexual Persons* at least acknowledges that, "It is quite true that the Biblical literature owes to the different epochs in which it was written . . . and that . . . the Church today addresses the Gospel to a world which differs in many ways from ancient days."[22] However, it nonetheless cites the consistency of biblical admonitions against homosexuality as "a solid foundation of Biblical testimony" along with the "Church's living tradition" as legitimately underpinning and warranting ongoing ecclesial condemnation of homosexuality.[23] To be

21. US Conference of Catholic Bishops, *Ministry Persons with Homosexual Inclination*, 4–5.

22. Congregation Doctrine of Faith, *Letter Pastoral Care of Homosexual Persons*, sec. 5.

23. Congregation Doctrine of Faith, *Letter Pastoral Care of Homosexual Persons*, sec. 5.

fair, this letter also affords at least a brief exposition of the wider scriptural contexts in which the admonitions are articulated. But it fails to sufficiently develop said wider context to illuminate the primary foci of the biblical authors which is not homosexuality per se but rather its association with idolatry and paganism (which the letter at least acknowledges) which are contrary to the Hebrew covenant with God and the Pauline notion of the kingdom of God.[24]

In citing the prohibition of homosexuality articulated in the Holiness Codes of Leviticus (Leviticus 18:22 and 20:13) the letter gives a nod to biblical sensitivities regarding conduct requisite for those belonging to the Chosen People of God. It does not, however, adequately convey the cultic rather than ethical concern of the biblical authors. Homosexuality is deemed to be an abomination (to'ebah) in Leviticus, employing a term which suggests abhorring something on religious and cultic grounds due to its association with idolatry which, in turn, defiled one so as to render them unclean for cultic participation.[25] Additionally, biblical admonitions against homosexuality were also informed by Near Eastern practices associated with fertility gods which were worshipped via ritually enacted temple-based sexual functions (kedeshim) (See Deuteronomy 23:17–18).[26] Hence, although the Hebrew Scripture condemns homosexual practice . . . a legitimate question, given the context of biblical admonitions, remains whether or not such prohibitions were sweeping ethical judgments, or were they deemed abominations because of their association with idolatry?[27] Biblical commentaries accentuate that these sexual instructions are proffered as a means to differentiate the Hebrew people from the Canaanites as the rightful custodians of the land which they came to occupy.[28] The underlying teaching behind these biblical sexual admonitions is a broader concern for covenanted relationship (hesed) with God, not the sexual acts proper.

Additionally, legitimate questions remain whether homosexuality is de facto absent from the living tradition of the church and whether

---

24. Congregation Doctrine of Faith, *Letter Pastoral Care of Homosexual Persons*, sec. 6.

25. Catholic Theological Society, *Human Sexuality*, 189.

26. Catholic Theological Society, *Human Sexuality*, 190.

27. Catholic Theological Society, *Human Sexuality*, 190.

28. Brown et al., *New Jerome Biblical Commentary*, 73–74; Chiu et al., *Paulist Biblical Commentary*, 115–6.

the understandings regarding human sexuality, sperm, and blood which marked the worldview of the ancient Hebrews resonates with the understandings and worldview regarding such things in the contemporary age. The contemporary age has benefitted from monumental growth of insights afforded by advances in biology, anatomy, physiology, medicine, psychology, sociology, etc. LGBTQ+ persons are members of the church, hence homosexuality is a part of the living tradition of the church. Furthermore, given the evolution in our understanding of human sexuality, few today would call for the exile of a married couple who has sex during a woman's menstrual cycle as called for by the same passages in Leviticus[29] utilized by ecclesial documents to condemn homosexuality. Context, culture, and historical understanding matter, and they shape, color, and inform moral sensitivities. This is true both in antiquity as well as now.

Likewise, in its mention of the prohibitions against homosexuality expressed in the Pauline tradition of the New Testament (I Corinthians 6:9, Romans 1:18–32, 1Timothy 1:9–10) the letter also acknowledges early Christianity's wider confrontation with the paganism of its day.[30] However, likewise, the letter fails to adequately consider the wider concern underlying the prohibition. Just as the Holiness Code of Leviticus was concerned about the demarcation of the Hebrew people as the people covenanted with God, the Pauline traditions are concerned with the followers of Jesus being demarcated by their association with the kingdom of God. Pagan prostitution was rampant at the time of Paul (particularly in Corinth), just as it was among the ancient Hebrews. In describing the Corinthian context to the early faith community in Rome, Paul juxtaposes those who are not of God's kingdom with those to whom Paul writes. Paul suggests that what differentiates them is relationship with God. Those not of the kingdom of God do not acknowledge God (Romans 1:23). They engage in idolatrous and pagan actions which in turn involve improper sexual conduct.[31] Here again the focus is not on sexual acts per se as it is on idolatry and right knowledge and relationship with God, i.e., on covenant/the kingdom of God. Within context, Paul is not proffering a condemnation of all homosexual activity per se, rather homosexuality that is chosen in opposition to a relationship

29. Leviticus 18:19, 20:18.

30. Congregation Doctrine of Faith, *Letter Pastoral Care of Homosexual Persons*, sec. 6.

31. Catholic Theological Society, *Human Sexuality*, 194–5, Brown et al., *New Jerome Biblical Commentary*, 835; Chiu et al., *Paulist Biblical Commentary*, 1242.

with God in favor for idols.[32] Again, context matters and of course not all contemporary LGBTQ+ persons exchange a relationship with God for idols. In fact, many LGBTQ+ persons live in relationships which point to and make present the steadfast covenantal love (*hesed*) of God, reveal the peace (*shalom*), justice (*mishpat*), and righteousness (*tzedakah*) of the kingdom, and the *kenotic* (self-sacrificial) and *agapic* (unconditional) love of Jesus. I think it also worth noting that Jesus offers no words concerning the issue of homosexuality. Indeed, as a button I was given as a gift suggests, "Jesus had two daddies and he turned out ok."

Within the midst of its presentation of what it deems to be scriptural underpinnings for the condemnation of homosexuality the Congregation for the Doctrine of Faith posits that, "Scripture cannot be properly understood when they are interpreted in a way which contradicts the Church's living Tradition."[33] It also asserts that scripture cannot stand without the magisterium of the church.[34] The Congregation goes so far as to suggest that those who interpret scripture differently reflect "a materialistic ideology which denies the transcendent nature of the human person as well as the supernatural vocation of every individual and are part of a movement which gives the impression that it represents all homosexual persons who are Catholics" and whose members ignore and seek to somehow undermine church teaching.[35] The Congregation further "makes it clear that departure from Church teaching on the matter of homosexuality in an effort to provide pastoral care is neither caring nor pastoral."[36]

I personally resent such characterization. A lifetime of study of Catholic theology and service to the Catholic Church affords me the right to have an opinion on matters and to listen to and consider alternative biblical interpretations. I do not espouse a materialistic ideology nor deny the transcendent nature of the human person. I do not deny the supernatural vocation of every individual. To the contrary, I believe that the students, colleagues, and friends who I mention above and in the introduction have

32. Catholic Theological Society, *Human Sexuality*, 195–6.

33. Congregation Doctrine of Faith, *Letter Pastoral Care of Homosexual Persons*, secs. 5, 8, 9.

34. Congregation Doctrine of Faith, *Letter Pastoral Care of Homosexual Persons*, secs. 5, 8, 9.

35. Congregation Doctrine of Faith, *Letter Pastoral Care of Homosexual Persons*, secs, 5, 8, 9.

36. Congregation Doctrine of Faith, *Letter Pastoral Care of Homosexual Persons*, sec.15; US Catholic Bishops, *Ministry Persons with Homosexual Inclination*, 13.

been called by God to relationship with God and to vocations within the church. I am not a part of any movement, nor do I claim to represent all LGBTQ+ Catholics. As evidenced by this very work and the engagement with a plethora of magisterial documents herein, it ought to be clear that I do not ignore church teaching. Nor do I seek to undermine church teaching. I wish for the church's teachings to be the best they can be via being precise in their language and terms. It is my desire to see the church's teachings marked by intellectual integrity. Above all, I want for the church's teachings to be a credible voice and witness of the example of Jesus. And, lastly, I write precisely because I do care and I do wish to offer pastoral compassion to those who are maltreated, such as the students, colleagues, and friends I have mentioned. This is what Jesus would do. One is certainly free to reject my interpretations and scholarship, but that does not afford one the right to call into question my motives, intentions, sincerity, and love for the church and all persons. My conscience, character, and care for others is not for the Congregation to judge.

HOMOSEXUALITY AND NATURAL LAW

In addition to utilizing scripture to condemn homosexual acts, Catholic tradition has consistently deemed homosexuality "intrinsically disordered" because the tradition has deemed homosexuality as a violation of natural law.[37] A synopsis of the tradition's argument against homosexuality in light of natural law goes like this: Natural law is human participation in the eternal law via the faculty of reason. Eternal law is the providential design of God imbued within the natural order ascertainable via reason. Inherent to the created order of nature one can utilize reason to discover that acts are ordered to *teloses*, i.e., ends/goods/goals. The sex act—only licit within the context of marriage—is directed toward the ends/goods of procreation (the procreative aspect/dimension), mutual consolation (pleasure, intimacy and friendship), and indissolubility (fidelity), which together are deemed the unitive aspects/dimensions. All acts of sex must be open to all three ends or goods and must never separate the procreative and unitive aspects and

---

37. *Catechism*, sec. 2357; US Catholic Bishops, *Ministry Persons with Homosexual Inclination*, 4; Also, for considerations of traditional and contemporary Natural Law, see Gula, "Natural Law Tradition" and "Natural Law Today," 220–230; Ryan, "Traditional Concept Natural Law," 413–427; Curran, "Natural Law Contemporary Moral Theology," 97–158.

dimensions if to be morally licit and in accord with the natural law. Historically within Catholic tradition disproportionate emphasis and focus was placed on the procreative end or good of sexual activity. This remains the case in the Church's contemporary consideration of homosexuality despite the fact that contemporary Catholic theology considering marriage recognizes the equal importance of all three ends/goods. In light of the aforesaid, it is maintained that homosexual sexual acts violate the natural law for they are deemed to not be open to the procreative end/good. They are also said to separate the unitive aspects/dimensions of sex from the procreative aspect/dimension for they do not occur within the context of marriage.

Experience reveals that LGBTQ+ persons are capable of being in relationships marked by mutual consolation and indissolubility (fidelity). Therefore, the focus for assessing the legitimacy of homosexual acts of sex centers upon the posited non-openness of these acts to procreation. In considering the church's natural law argument in opposition to homosexual acts two points are problematic, namely the tradition's tendency to consider natural law from a physicalist point of view and its equation of procreation to reproduction and education of an offspring.

Physicalism vs. Personalism

St. Thomas Aquinas gives voice to the Catholic tradition's most widely held understanding of the natural law, one perpetuated throughout magisterial teachings on sexuality. Thomas was influenced by Stoic assumptions regarding sex, namely that sex pursued for pleasure outside of the purpose of procreation is an offense against nature for emotions are part of human beings' lower sphere requiring control by the higher sphere of human beings, namely reason and will.[38] Additionally, Thomas was also influenced by a third century Roman lawyer, Ulpian. Ulpian defined natural law as that which nature teaches all animals, as opposed to the law of humanity which pertains to laws which are proper only to human beings. Such laws pertain to the rational aspect of humanity.[39] Defining the natural law as being common to human beings and animals results in a tendency to identify human actions as mere animal or biological processes or functions, i.e., to reduce the morality of human acts to the physical structure and/or biological

38. Kosnik et al., *Human Sexuality*, 198; Modras, "Pope John Paul II's Theology of the Body," 150.

39. Kosnik et al., *Human Sexuality*, 106–7.

function of the act apart from human reason and relationships.[40] Contemporary moral theologians such as Richard Gula, SS, describe such an approach to natural law as physicalism, i.e., "the tendency in moral analysis to emphasize, or even to absolutize, the physical and biological aspects of the human person and human actions independently of the function of reason and freedom."[41] To put it crudely, when it comes to sexual morality, natural law physicalism tends to reduce human beings to penises and sperm, and vaginas and ovaries, and the functions associated with them. Morality becomes a matter of conforming human structures and functions to a blueprint inherent in nature—deemed to be God's rule—which exists in a state, design, and pattern not influenced by the intervention of human reason.[42] Such an approach, one that has historically dominated Catholic natural law teaching, is one that fails to do justice to those aspects of human beings which makes them uniquely human and the image and likeness of God, namely reason, will, conscience, and relationality. This despite the fact that Aquinas noted that it was reason that enabled human beings to participate in the eternal law and which inclines human beings to want to know the whole of reality so as to come to truth.[43]

Contemporary moral theology seeks to give due attention to the complexity of the human person (we are more than anatomical body parts or biological functions) and to overcome the reductionist anthropology of a physicalist approach to natural law. Contemporary approaches grant greater attention to the particularly human faculties of reason and will for, in the words of Gula, "insofar as humans are rational, whatever pertains to reason belongs to the natural law. This includes the tendency toward truth and cooperating with one another in a social existence."[44] As Gula describes, this type of approach to natural law is called personalism, i.e., an "emphasis on dimensions of the human person and human actions which extend beyond the physical and biological to include the social, spiritual and psychological dimensions as well."[45] A personalist approach to natural law does not

---

40. Curran, *Contemporary Moral Problems*, 107–110.

41. Gula, *Reason Informed by Faith*, 226.

42. Gula, *Reason Informed by Faith*, 227.

43. Gula, *Reason Informed by Faith*, 224.

44. Gula, *Reason Informed by Faith*, 226; For consideration of the human person as more broadly understood, see Gula, "Human Person," 63–74; Gula, "Moral Decision Making," 304–306; Himes, "Human Person in Contemporary Theology," 49–62.

45. Gula, *Reason Informed by Faith*, 226.

view nature as something fixed and closed off to or beyond human creative development. As Gula explains, it is an approach that maintains that the human person can "creatively intervene to direct the natural law in a way that is properly proportionate to full human development. The "nature" which reason explores is no longer separated from the total complexity of personal, human life taken in all its relationships."[46] A personalist approach to natural law takes reason, not the physical structure of human faculties or actions, as the standard of natural law. According to Gula, it identifies the "natural" with "the total complexity of human reality taken in all its relationships" and "respects the creative human capacity for knowledge and freedom."[47] It takes into consideration human experience and relationships as being constitutive aspects of our human endeavor to discover what it means to be good, to be human.[48] Underlying the contemporary shift from a physicalist approach to natural law to a personalist approach are corresponding shifts in world views/theological methodologies and an evolving anthropology operative in Catholic thought.

Classical Essentialism vs. Historical Existentialism

Within the teachings of the Second Vatican Council one can detect a shift in theological thinking/methodologies, or a shift in world views.[49] Prior to Vatican II the operative world view inherent to Roman Catholic theology was a Classical, or Essentialistic, world view. Accompanying Vatican II's sensitivity to history comes what may be described as a Historical Existential world view.[50] Traditional Classical Essentialism was a world view based upon a metaphysical dualism. It posited the existence of a higher world and a transcendent absolute from which everything came and to which everything returned. The function of theology was to define and explain revealed truths (truths regarding the higher reality); to defend orthodox doctrines and condemn false ones; and to teach revealed truths with unquestionable authority. Theology was deductive in nature, working from the absolutes

---

46. Gula, *Reason Informed by Faith*, 233, 235.

47. Gula, *Reason Informed by Faith*, 235, 240.

48. Gula, *Reason Informed by Faith*, 241, 243.

49. Gula, *Reason Informed by Faith*, 25–40; Curran, *Contemporary Problems in Moral Theology*, 116–42.

50. Tkacik and McGonigle, *Pneumatic Correctives*, 7.

of the higher reality and seeking to have the temporal conform to these realities as if they were a metaphysical blueprint for human conduct. Such a world view enabled the church and its theology to voyage through history yet remain unchanged by history, for the church belonged more properly to the substance of the higher reality. The church was not subject to the world or worldly cultures because its essence was at one with the absolute, perfect, immutable, and eternal metaphysical higher reality. The church was viewed to be superior to and over and above the world and human cultures.[51] R. Kevin Seasoltz, OSB, summarized the characteristics of the Classical Essentialist world view succinctly and with clarity:

> A Classicist world view of culture maintains that there is but one culture which is normative, universal and permanent. The values it embraces and the meanings it communicates are universal in claim and scope. It appeals to an abstract ideal and its concerns are unchanging; it attends to universals rather than particulars. It is informed by classical philosophy . . . and issues laws which are universally applicable and truths which are eternal. Circumstances of time and place are accidental . . . Humanity itself is a universal concept reflecting an unchanging reality . . . When a Classicist understanding of culture prevails, theology is looked upon as a permanent achievement.[52]

The Classical world view stands at odds with the vision of Vatican II which tended toward a Historical Existential world view marked by a vision of the church that emphasized an openness to worldly cultures, a universal mission, and the task of *aggiornamento* (updating, renewing, adapting according to the signs of the times).[53] Vatican II recognized that it belonged to the church's very essence to change. It was the church's responsibility to learn from various cultural forms of history and to apply what it learns to ecclesial reform. The shift toward a Historical Existential theological paradigm at Vatican II was primarily the result of the Council's attempt to direct theology to where people are, i.e., their lived experience, so as to be meaningful and viable to them. A Historical Existential world view recognizes that each culture has distinct sets of values and meanings. Heavily influenced by contemporary social sciences, the Historical Existential view

---

51. Tkacik and McGonigle, *Pneumatic Correctives*, 7.

52. Seasoltz, "Sacred Liturgy," 54.

53. *Lumen Gentium*, secs. 9, 13, 17, 48; *Gaudium et Spes*, secs. 39, 40, 44, 53, 57, 58, 62; *Ad Gentes Divinitus*, secs. 2, 16, 22.

recognizes the historical and relative character of the communication of meaning and values and, thus, that they are open to change. It attempts to understand principles as they operate in changing contexts, not as abstract, static entities. The focus is on particulars, not universals. It is marked by inductive reasoning, moving from the lived experiences of people to assertions of truth. Development is seen as the product of human history, not providentialism or the manifestation of some metaphysical type. Theology in this world view is conceived of as an ongoing process to be carried out in the context of human experiences. The church is not viewed as existing for itself over and above the world, but as existing for and amid all of humanity. The challenge of ecclesiology becomes reading the signs of the times so as to discover new ways to respond to the everchanging gift of God's self-disclosure to humanity.[54]

A physicalist approach to natural law is informed by and flows forth from a Classical Essentialist world view and theological methodology. A personalist approach to natural law is informed by and flows forth from a Historical Existential world view and theological methodology. As Charles Curran notes, Classical Essentialism utilizes a theological methodology which "tends to be abstract, *a priori*, and deductive. It wants to cut through the concrete circumstances to arrive at the abstract essence, which is always true, and then works with these abstract universal essences."[55] A Historical Existential world view utilizes a theological methodology which considers concrete, particular, and individual historical and existential circumstances in discerning what is reality and in striving to identify immutable essences. According to Curran, "it tends to be concrete, *a posteriori*, and inductive," moving tentatively from observations and experiences as it proceeds to conclusions.[56] Classical Essentialism tends to be legalistic, whereas Historical Existentialism tends to accentuate rational deliberation.[57] Consequently, when addressing homosexuality a Classical Essentialistic approach to natural law condemns homosexual acts on the basis of a deduction drawn from what is deemed to be an absolute and immutable law inherent in nature, namely that all sex acts must be open to the procreation and education of offspring. Such an approach does not take into consideration other aspects of the lived human experience and moral deliberation. Morality is a matter

54. Tkacik and McGonigle, *Pneumatic Correctives*, 8–11.

55. Curran, *Contemporary Problems in Moral Theology*, 119.

56. Curran, *Contemporary Problems in Moral Theology*, 119.

57. Curran, *Contemporary Problems in Moral Theology*, 105.

of conforming to nature. A Historical Existential consideration of homosexuality would call for consideration of how lived human experience, reason, intention, context/circumstances, consequences, and relationships shed light on the morality of homosexual acts. It recognizes that human beings in the contemporary scientific and technological age are able to interact with nature so as to influence nature towards the good of human beings.[58] Classical Essentialism tends to reduce the reality of human sexuality to its physical function. Historical Existentialism tends to examine human sexuality within the wider context of the complexus of what it means to be human. Classical Essentialism is resistant of change. Historical Existentialism is open to change in light of human relationships, growth, and development. Morality in a Classicist approach is a matter of conforming to an unchanging pattern/design inherent in nature. A Historical Existential approach sees morality as a constitutive aspect of the human vocation whereby we seek meaning within the context of our life experiences and relationships.[59]

HOMOSEXUALITY AND PROCREATION?

Utilizing a Historical Existential and personalist approach to natural law, we can consider homosexual acts more broadly than in terms of function, rather vis-à-vis sexual functions in light of the total complexus of what it means to be human. Again, we human beings are more than the functions of our anatomical parts and biological processes. We are also rational, volitional, and relational creatures. Experience shows that homosexual persons are capable of meeting the unitive aspects/dimensions of human sexuality, i.e., they are able to live in mutually consoling (*kenotic* and *agapic* love marked by care, compassion, and friendship) and indissoluble (faithfully committed and covenanted) relationships. So what of the procreative end/good/aspect/dimension of human sexuality? Can homosexuals and homosexual acts be open to this?

Given that the focus of morality is to be love, faithfulness, and relationships—as conveyed by the scriptural emphases on covenant, the kingdom of God, and example of Jesus—and is to be discerned utilizing the totality of human faculties, experience, and relationships, then one must consider homosexuality more broadly than in terms of sexual functions

58. Curran, *Contemporary Problems in Moral Theology*, 112–3.
59. Curran, *Contemporary Problems in Moral Theology*, 117–35.

alone. Homosexuality needs to be considered more broadly than in terms of the sex act exclusively examined in terms of procreation and education of offspring. When it comes to homosexuality, the unitive ends/goods of sex are not the issue—procreation is. Can homosexuality be said to be open to procreation?

If we consider procreation more broadly than offspring, then I maintain that the answer to the question above is yes. As Christians we believe that the gospel has the power and ability to draw people to it. It is our responsibility to live in such a way that the gospel is made manifest, i.e., that our lives point to and make present the love that God has for humanity and that Jesus has for the church. This is what it means for the church to be a sacrament. If we live in relationships which point to and make present the covenanted love that God has for humanity (*hesed*) and that Jesus has for the church (*kenotic* and *agapic*) the gospel is incarnated in our temporal witness and experience. Via such relationships we become exemplars of the love of God, the love of Jesus, and the gospel. As such, human relationships marked by such love have the power and ability to draw others to God and Jesus. Such relationships, therefore, can be said to be procreative.

Since LGBTQ+ persons witness such love, they too can be said to honor the procreative end/good/aspect/dimension of human sexuality. Additionally, they can be said to be in relationships that are also educational, for they are able to be a domestic church affording an example and witness of God's and Jesus' love to the wider community which, in turn, edifies all of us. Viewed in this light, LGBTQ+ relationships are no different from heterosexual relationships which have not produced offspring. The gay students, colleagues, and friends that I discussed above and in the introduction have all afforded me an example of God's and Jesus' love. They have all taught me much about what it means to be a Christian. They have all edified my relationship with God. And they all build up the church via the ministries they provide. In short, they can be said to procreative in this more broadly understood sense.

The Catholic tradition is ripe full of examples of love that are procreative in this broader sense. The Trinity itself is understood to be a community of persons. It is through the love exchanged between God and Jesus that the Spirit proceeds. In turn, it is from the love of the Spirit that the church is born. Neither Jesus nor his mother engaged in sexual love but it certainly would not be suggested that their witness and example of love was not procreative. Heterosexual marriages that do not yield offspring are not deemed an affront to the procreative end/good. The witness of innumerable virgins and celibates throughout the history of the church have afforded the church examples of love which are procreative in the broader sense. Furthermore, our contemporary American experience affords us the lived witness and examples of gay couples who have adopted children and who have raised them in loving and caring environs. Therefore, it is time for the church to cease characterizing the love shared by faithfully committed LGBTQ+ persons as "non-genuine, self-indulgent and devoid of authentic affection and complementarity." It is time for the church to recognize that LGBTQ+ relationships can be procreative. When? Now.

HOMOSEXUALITY AND CHRISTIAN ANTHROPOLOGY

Along with the evolving developments in the area of biblical scholarship, moral theology, and ecclesial tradition have come an evolving and developing notion of Christian anthropology. Above, we have already seen how the Catholic tradition, vis-à-vis sexual ethics, has historically tended to reduce the human person to our biological functions. Likewise, we have seen that contemporary theology emphasizes that the human person is much more than anatomical parts and biological processes/functions. Christian anthropology must view the human person in light of the total complexus of what it means to be human—rational, volitional, spiritual, psychological, historical, contextual, cultural, relational, etc.[60] It is true that we human beings are embodied beings and that who we are is communicated and expressed through/via our bodies. However, it still remains for us to discover the innermost subjective interiority of the human person which lies within us and which the body makes known. We are not to equate the innermost interior subjectivity of the human person with bodily expression alone.

When one examines Pope John Paul II's "theology of the body" addresses and work, *The Acting Person*, there is a shift to appreciating the interior subjectivity and broader realities of what constitutes a human being. Yet there remains a focus on the human being in terms of the body and its functions, i.e., what is deemed a "nuptial" meaning of the body evidenced by anatomical and biological complementarity of the sexes which accentuates anew the procreative aspect/dimension of human sexuality. According

---

60. For consideration of the human person as more broadly understood, see Gula, *Reason Informed by Faith*, 63–74, 304–306; Himes, "Human Person in Contemporary Theology," 49–62.

to Richard Grecco, "John Paul II interprets Genesis 1 as an objective description of sexuality (as if it were history) and in his view it is impossible to understand our present historical state without referring to our fundamental state of innocence."[61] As human beings move out of solitude and search for identity we are moved toward relationships. We express our deeper interior subjective selves via/through our bodies and discover that our ultimate fulfillment can only be realized in mutual enrichment.[62] The pope deems that this mutual enrichment can only be realized via the sexual complementarity of male and female and that this eventuating relationship renders us the image and likeness of God.[63] Any other relationship alienates one from oneself and fails to afford one the communal relationship which enables one's interior subjectivity to be authentically expressed.[64] In light of this, an anthropology derived from a historical reading of the Genesis account would, therefore, render homosexual relationships as deviations from God's providential created designs for human sexuality. Such relationships are, therefore, ultimately deviations from the natural order and impediments to authentically communicating one's interior subjectivity. They do not allow for the realization of appropriate human communion. They reduce the body to an object separate from the subjective interiority of the person.[65]

Additionally, Grecco notes that the pope speaks of human emotions and feelings as something to be dominated and subordinated by the rational will. Here the late pope is echoing a Platonic dualism and Stoic sensitivities which view the body and passions with suspicion and as aspects of our lower human appetites which need to be controlled by our higher faculties of intellect and will so as to become compliant tools of the soul.[66] Ultimately the pope views the sexual urge as a force of nature whose natural end is procreation and, therefore, any sexual act not open to said end is paramount to using another person as a means to an end rather than an end in itself. The conclusion, therefore, is that sexual expression disassociated from procreation is evil.[67]

61. Grecco, "Recent Ecclesiastical Teaching," 138, 153.

62. Grecco, "Recent Ecclesiastical Teaching," 139.

63. Grecco, "Recent Ecclesiastical Teaching," 139–140.

64. Grecco, "Recent Ecclesiastical Teaching," 141–2.

65. Grecco, "Recent Ecclesiastical Teaching," 142.

66. Grecco, "Recent Ecclesiastical Teaching," 150.

67. Grecco, "Recent Ecclesiastical Teaching," 151–2.

By constructing an anthropology through an historical reading of the mythical paradigm of the Genesis account the pope posits an historical state of innocence and interprets the original nakedness of Adam and Eve as evidence of human beings' original self-mastery and self-control over our sexual organs capable of "disinterested" self-giving and devoid of any taint of selfish enjoyment.[68] The loss of original innocence caused by the sin and fall of human beings rendered a constitutive break between the original unity of interiority and body as evidenced by concupiscence. Human beings are left imbalanced and distorted, directing sexuality to lust and appropriation of others as objects rather than towards the sincere self-giving gift of oneself to another and towards procreation.[69] Again, Grecco observes within the late pope's framework:

> . . . Homosexuality is the result of sin. God simply could not, would not, and did not create homosexuals as such. The homosexual condition is the result of the first sin, an aspect . . . of concupiscence . . . sexual attraction or desire for someone of the same sex is a disorder . . . sexuality was created for procreation, not enjoyment . . . homosexual acts . . . are the antithesis of such (disinterested self-giving) love.[70]

Ultimately, even as Pope John Paul II and contemporary Catholic theology have striven to balance the three ends/goods of marriage and to expand its anthropology by recognizing the wider total complexus of what it means to be a human being, the end results remain the same. The result is a non-critical reading of scripture which interprets a mythical narrative paradigm as being historical utilized so as to proffer contemporary condemnations and a reduction of human sexuality to procreation. Such a result deems aspects such as passion and emotion which edify mutual consolation as sinful and evil (therefore, ultimately inconsistent with the contemporary efforts towards balancing the sexual ends/goods). Utilizing scripture in such a manner is inconsistent with the teachings of *Dei Verbum* and distorts that which is mythic and paradigmatic by equating it with history. The only experience we human beings know is the one that we have. Our experience is what is natural. Thus, juxtaposing our human experience to a conjectured alternative pre-fallen state of innocence with a corresponding view of nature not touched by human beings is paramount

---

68. Grecco, "Recent Ecclesiastical Teaching," 154–5.

69. Grecco, "Recent Ecclesiastical Teaching," 154.

70. Grecco, "Recent Ecclesiastical Teaching," 154–5.

to creating a conjectured idealized state of nature. This ideal, in turn, is employed so as to render punitive and condemning judgments upon human beings and nature as experienced. There is no meaningful nature other than the one we human beings experience.

Sexuality entails more than procreation. Procreation can be understood as being more than offspring. Contemporary theology, the other social sciences, and personal experience acknowledge that not all passion and emotion is sinful or evil, nor impediments to healthy sexual self-giving of oneself to another. To the contrary, passion and emotion can be experienced as enhancing mutual consolation and thus, in turn, of lending to fidelity (indissolubility). Consequently, the pope's condemnation of sexuality is no more compelling than the ecclesial condemnations which have preceded it. Furthermore, it is relationality which constitutes human beings as the image and likeness of God, not sexual activity. The Genesis account the pope references deems human beings the image and likeness of God once there is a community of persons, once there is relationality, prior to the mandate to be procreative.

BUILDING A BRIDGE FOR THE LGBTQ+ COMMUNITY

Fr. James Martin, SJ, suggests, and I agree, that what is needed in the American church today are bridges between the church and the LGBTQ+ community.[71] Groundwork for such bridges could begin with the church practicing what it preaches. Martin suggests that the church could treat LGBTQ+ persons with "respect, compassion and sensitivity." It could recognize the gifts they have for the church. The church could listen to their concerns and provide ministries in service to them. It could end all ecclesial discrimination *ad intra* against LGBTQ+ persons. As this work was being written the Supreme Court of the United States rendered a judgment making it illegal to discriminate against LGBTQ+ persons in the workplace.[72] The church could cease using language which disparages, debases, and wounds LGBTQ+ persons. The church needs to be in solidarity with its LGBTQ+ members, encountering and accompanying them as persons, not

71. See Martin, *Building a Bridge*.

72. See deVogue and Cole, "Supreme Court Says Federal Law Protects LGBTQ Workers."

categories. This is what Jesus would do. The church needs to put relationships and community before condemnation.[73]

Martin posits that respect for the LGBTQ+ community would entail that they be included in the church as the baptized members of the people of God they are. Members of the said community could be identified and called by the terminology they prefer. Their gifts of compassion, perseverance, forgiveness, holiness, and ministerial evangelism be acknowledged. Their place within the workplace be safe guarded.[74] Compassion for the LGBTQ+ community would mean for the church to listen to the community. It would mean for the church to experience their suffering with them. The church would defend LGBTQ+ persons and speak out against the discrimination, abuse, and bullying they so often experience.[75] Sensitivity toward the LGBTQ+ community would require that the church become aware of the feelings of LGBTQ+ persons and to come to know and accompany them as friends.[76]

If we, the church, do these things we will be more able to hear what the Spirit is saying and discern if a pneumatic corrective regarding ecclesial teachings on homosexuality is being asked of us. Doing this would be to emulate the example of Jesus who always sought to encounter persons where they were and who frequently went to the margins of society to do so. Jesus welcomed tax collectors, women, Gentiles, Samaritans, prostitutes, lepers, sick, possessed, and blind persons. Although we are all sinners and may be inclined to think that we are not worthy for Jesus to receive us/enter under our roof, Jesus does. And Jesus proactively seeks us out to do so. We must do the same for one another. As Father Martin observes, "the work of God cannot be accomplished if one part of the church is essentially separated from any other part."[77] It is worth noting that the gospels reveal that it is the likes of the marginalized who are drawn into table fellowship and relationship with Jesus. Those who are so rigorously legalistic so as to make laws, rules, regulations, social customs and mores absolute, rather than relationships, are the ones who remain unreconciled with Jesus and God.

73. See Martin, "We need to build a bridge."

74. Martin, *Building a Bridge*, 25–33.

75. Martin, *Building a Bridge*, 36–41.

76. Martin, *Building a Bridge*, 43–47.

77. Martin, *Building a Bridge*, 15.

Conclusion

In the aftermath of the 2016 Pulse Nightclub shooting in Orlando, Florida, Bishop Robert Lynch of St. Petersburg, Florida, blogged:

> . . . sadly it is religion, including our own, which targets, mostly verbally, and also often breeds contempt for gays, lesbians and transgender people. Attacks today on LGBT men and women often plant the seed of contempt, then hatred, which can ultimately lead to violence. Those women and men who were mowed down early yesterday morning were all made in the image and likeness of God. We teach that. We should believe that. We must stand for that.[78]

Bishop Lynch was right and the time for the church to acknowledge how its language, attitudes, and disposition towards gays does sow seeds of contempt, hatred, and violence is now. When? Now. As The United States Conference of Catholic Bishops rightly proclaims, "God does not love someone any less because he/she is homosexual. God's love is always and everywhere offered to all those who are open to receive it."[79]

As a community tasked with pointing to and making present God's love to all, the church must accept the LGBTQ+ community in a manner that reflects that love. In short, as Martin asserts, "people must be accepted, as Jesus accepted them. When a person comes before Jesus, Jesus will surely not say, 'Go away because you're homosexual.'"[80]

---

78. Lynch, "It is Religion, including our own, which Targets Gay People."

79. See US Catholic Bishops, *Always Our Children*.

80. Martin, *Building a Bridge*, 47.

3

ECUMENISM AND INTERRELIGIOUS DIALOGUE

LIFE EXPERIENCE

As I HAVE SHARED elsewhere in the book I am a member of an ecumenical family. My wife is Protestant (a member of the Evangelical Lutheran Church in America) and I am Roman Catholic. Over the 29 years of our married life we have worshipped with one another in our respective traditions and exposed our three sons to both traditions as well. Hence, for me, in addition to being a theological and pastoral interest on the professional level given my passionate commitment to the Second Vatican Council, my commitment to ecumenism is also very personal. Ecumenism strives to restore unity among the various expressions of Christianity. As I was praying about and discerning the topics that I wished to address in this book ecumenism was placed on my heart and mind by the Spirit.

Roman Catholicism made revolutionary, doctrine changing,[1] advances in the cause of ecumenism and interreligious dialogue at the Second Vatican Council and has continued to further the causes in the decades

---

1. Rush, *Vision of Vatican* II, 477–8. Father Rush references and quotes both Sullivan, "Vatican II and the Postconciliar Magisterium," and O'Collins, *Second Vatican Council on Other Religions,* who both deem Vatican II's teachings regarding the salvific value of other religions as constituting a change and/or development of doctrine in official Catholic teaching as well praxis.

which have followed.[2] Interreligious dialogue is a commitment to discerning God's activity in religions outside of Christianity. When is the time for these advances to be known and the ethical imperative[3] they connote to be lived by the Catholic faithful? When? Now.

I know that our family situation is not unique. There are many families that are comprised of members who come from and worship at varying religious traditions and institutions. Additionally, the numerous deacons I have taught over the past two and a half decades are routinely presiding over sacraments (baptism and marriage) and funeral rites which require that they minister to people of a myriad of faiths. And, as our world becomes ever more interconnected, all of us are afforded opportunities to encounter and be in relationship with persons of other faiths.

If I found the chapter on homosexuality to be the most challenging, I found this chapter to be the least challenging. This is mainly because of the lived witness of my wife and all that she has shared with me ever since our courting days as undergraduates at Auburn University. Suzy and I met shortly after I left a Catholic seminary. I had gone to seminary after many years of discerning the possibility that God might be calling me to the Catholic priesthood. My hope was that the seminary would afford me an environment in which to continue my discernment, accompanied by daily prayer and worship, spiritual direction, ministerial service opportunities, and academic study which would, in turn, better illuminate what God was calling me to. What I got instead was a seminary environment marked by dysfunctionality and unhealthiness, and one which turned the sacramental life into battlegrounds for varying ideologies. Rather than illuminating God's presence in my life seminary shrouded me in darkness and threatened the very faith that had led me to enter. I left seminary in deep anguish and pain with my faith severely wounded. Suzy would be my Saint Monica.

Suzy is my prophetess. God utilizes her to illuminate God's will for me and to speak God's truth to me. After months of friendship as undergraduates I fell in love with her. I had to discern if God's will for me was to be

---

2. It is simply not possible to denote the plethora of advances made in the areas of ecumenical and interreligious dialogue between the Catholic Church and other Christian religions subsequent to the Second Vatican Council. For an overview of advances, see Cassidy, *Rediscovering Vatican II*; Pontifical Council for the Promotion of Christian Unity; Pontifical Council for Inter-religious Dialogue.

3. Rush, *Vision of Vatican II*, 461–2. Father Rush references Knitter, "*Nostra Aetate*: A Milestone in the History of Religions," which suggests that *Nostra Aetate* established dialogue with other religions as an "obligation" and "ethical responsibility" for Catholics.

her husband rather than a priest. This discernment was challenging for I left seminary largely because of the unhealthiness of the particular place where I attended, not because I had come to resolution regarding a possible priestly vocation. It was the faith (Protestant) and witness of Suzy that saved my own faith (Catholic) as she afforded me the greatest example of God's love and the joy of faith I had ever witnessed (and this remains true to this day) and as she insisted that I not abandon my Catholic faith, the Catholic Church, nor the academic study of Catholic theology. The faith and witness of this Protestant girl would be what illuminated God's will for me and what would inform and sustain my vocation as a Catholic theologian and teacher then, over the years, and now. As Saint Monica did for her son, Saint Augustine, Suzy saved my Catholic faith, illuminated God's will for me, and sustained me in my vocation via her constant prayers and witness of faith and God's love.

God certainly has a sense of humor. In the midst of my anguishing discernment, of all the people God could have brought into my life, God brought an eighteen-year-old Protestant girl with a faith, joy, and love of the likes I have never experienced . . . with the maiden name of "Priest." I can recall when God invited me to open myself to discerning a vocation of marital love with Suzy rather than returning to another seminary. I phoned my mother and told her that I was going to marry a "priest" instead of becoming one. And that is what I did. And because I did my Catholic faith survived. Not only did my faith survive the aftermath of a troubling seminary experience, because of Suzy's life-long prayers, witness, support, and love, my Catholic faith and vocation have persevered. Her Protestantism saved and edified my Catholicism. I am able to echo both Saint Peter and Pope John Paul II who said, respectively:

> I begin to see how true it is that God shows no partiality. Rather, the person of any nation who fears God and acts uprightly is acceptable to God (Acts 10:34–35).
> At the Second Vatican Council, the Catholic Church committed Herself irrevocably to following the path of the ecumenical venture . . .[4]

Together with my experience with Suzy, it is this irrevocable commitment to ecumenism that the Holy Spirit called the Catholic Church to at the Second Vatican Council that additionally rendered this chapter the least challenging. For the first time in the history of the twenty one ecumenical

4. John Paul II, *Ut Unum Sint,* sec. 3.

councils of Catholic Christianity, God's self-revelation to all people is explicitly acknowledged, the positive aspects inherent in other religions affirmed, and Catholics called upon to dialogue with them.[5] Praise be to God, since Vatican II the Catholic Church has made herculean efforts toward and proffered a plethora of graced contributions to the cause of ecumenism for which I am grateful, appreciative, and proud.[6] Indeed, in the *Decree on Ecumenism* (*Unitatis Redintegratio*) the Council posited that: "The restoration of unity among all Christians is one of the principal concerns of the Second Vatican Council . . . division openly contradicts the will of Christ, scandalizes the world, and damages the most holy cause–the preaching of the Gospel to every creature . . ." (*Unitatis Redintegratio*, section 1).

Furthermore, as Paul Knitter notes, "Vatican II . . . did something that had never been done before in the official statements of the church, it recognized and affirmed in other religions elements that are true and good (*Lumen Gentium*, section 16), precious things, both religious and human (*Gaudium et* Spes, section 92), elements of truth and grace (*Ad Gentes Divinitus*, section 9), spiritual and moral goods (*Nostra Aetate*, section 2), seeds of the Word (*Ad Gentes Divinitus*, sections 11 and 15), rays of that truth which illuminate all humankind (*Nostra Aetate*, section 2)."[7] In light of such affirmation of other religions the Council calls upon all Catholics "to prudently and lovingly engage in dialogue with other believers" (*Nostra Aetate*, section 2).[8] Subsequent to the Second Vatican Council ecumenical and interreligious dialogue have been deemed by subsequent popes and magisterial teachings to be essential to the church's mission.[9]

The combination of Suzy and the Council have brought me to a place where I have become intolerant of intolerance and where I do not accept theological hubris, nor mean-spirited theology. When we married I was not willing to ask Suzy to do for me—promise to expose and rear our children to/in the Catholic faith—what I was not willing to reciprocate and do for her in return. This is what ecumenism and interreligious dialogue call for— a dialectic of mutual respect, exposure, and dialogue marked by humility and love which opens oneself to the mysteries and graces of God that God might illuminate and afford you via encounter with another. Ecumenical

5. Rush, *Vision of Vatican II*, 475–8.

6. See Pontifical Commission for the Promotion of Christian Unity.

7. Knitter, "Bridge or Boundary," 261.

8. Knitter, "Bridge or Boundary," 262.

9. See Madges, *Vatican II Forty Years Later.*

and interreligious dialogue demand that all sides recognize the authenticity and shortcomings of themselves as well as each other (See *Unitatis Redintegratio* sections 4 and 9). Via dialogue we come to know more about ourselves as well as the other. We must allow ourselves to mutually expand one another's knowledge and enrichment and allow ourselves to be questioned, challenged, and corrected.[10]

Conversation opens one up and leads to greater understanding. For conversation to be authentic one must be open to presenting oneself as well as be open to the risk to one's understanding in face of the other. One must share one's underlying assumptions and prejudices as well as be open to changing one's perspective. Ecumenism and interreligious dialogue enrich one's faith, broaden one's understanding of God, and deepen one's relationships with God and others.[11] Hostility or indifference towards the cause of ecumenism and interreligious dialogue impoverishes one's faith, limits one's understanding of God, and compromises one's relationship with God for it violates what Jesus prayed for. As Pope Francis reminds us: "Commitment to ecumenism responds to the prayer of the Lord Jesus that "they may all be one" (Jn 17:21)."[12]

Yves Congar, OP, conveys the spirit of dialogue beautifully in his work, *Divided Christendom*:

> Ecumenism begins when it is admitted that others, not only individuals but ecclesiastical bodies as well, may also be right though they differ from us; that they too have truth, holiness, and gifts of God even though they do not profess our form of Christianity. There is ecumenism . . . when it is believed that others are Christian not in spite of their particular confession but in it and by it. Such conviction governs that complex of ideas which make up the ecumenical attitude—respect for other confessions and the action of the Holy Spirit in them, the sense and the avowal of the past sins, limitations and failures of one's own confession, the desire to know about other confessions and the gifts of God to them and to enter into friendly relations with them, pending full unity, as far as possible into effective communion.[13]

---

10. Madges, *Vatican II Forty Years Later,* 266.

11. Rush, *Vision of Vatican II,* 373–4.

12. Francis, *Evangelium Gaudium,* sec. 244.

13. Congar, *Divided Christendom,* 373–4.

A Sign of the Times and Inspired Departure from the Past

The two popes who oversaw the proceedings of the Second Vatican Council, popes John XXIII and Paul VI, viewed ecumenism and interreligious dialogue as signs of the times illuminated by the Holy Spirit which the church was being called to address at the Council. Prior to the Council, in 1960, Pope John XXIII established a new office within the Roman Curia, the Secretariat for the Promotion of Christian Unity (SCU), headed by Cardinal Augustine Bea, charged with keeping the ecumenical priority at the forefront of the Council's agenda. As the Council unfolded this office would facilitate the participation of ecumenical observers, advise the pope and various conciliar commissions, and was ultimately empowered to act as a conciliar commission in its own right with the authority to draft documents.

Additionally, in 1964 Pope Paul VI created a department within the Roman Curia for relations with peoples of other religions originally known as the Secretariat for Non-Christians and renamed the Pontifical Council for Interreligious Dialogue in 1988. From the opening of the Council Pope John spoke at length about the unity of the Christian and human family that he sought to promote through the Council. As the Council unfolded Pope Paul VI gave the SCU permission to work on the schema specifically dedicated to ecumenism to be presented to the Council and which he ultimately promulgated.[14]

This schema took its cue from the ecumenical movements of the previous quarter century. Said movements were largely the work of Protestant and Anglican missionaries, the patriarch of Constantinople (head of the Orthodox Churches), and the World Council of Churches. Consequently, the new schema had the tone of the Catholic Church opening itself up to unprecedented and unparalleled dialogue with the separated brethren, for the Catholic Church had previously taken a non-involvement approach to the movement. According to scholar Francine Cardman, "Prior to the Second Vatican Council ecumenical activity on the part of Roman Catholics had very nearly been anathema. Repeatedly, Rome had refused invitations and forbidden participation in the early ecumenical conferences."[15]

14. For an overview of the history of Roman Catholicism's participation in the ecumenical movement and background to the ecumenical and interreligious teachings of the Second Vatican Council, see Cassidy, *Rediscovering Vatican II*.

15. Cardman, "One Treasure Only," 176; Rush, *The Vision of Vatican II*, 375–88.

For centuries, the Catholic understanding of unity followed a "return" motif, i.e., restoration of Christian unity could only be achieved by separated churches returning to the Roman Catholic Church. Although Orthodox and Protestant efforts towards ecumenism intensified in the years after the two world wars Roman Catholic participation continued to be forbidden and the cause of ecumenical unity deemed by the Catholic Church to be a wayward Protestant affair promoting a false Christianity marked by error and illusion.[16]

Therefore, it has been said that Vatican II inaugurated an inspired departure from preceding Catholic approaches to ecumenism as the Council established ecumenism and the restoration of Christian unity as one of its principal aims/goals.[17] According to *Unitatis Redintegratio*, "The restoration of unity among all Christians is one of the principal concerns of the Second Vatican Council."[18]

A foundational principle for the Council's ecumenical commitment was the growing acknowledgement that grace and vestiges/elements of the church of Christ were present in other Christian communities and, thus, in some measure, those communities participate in the one church of Christ.

> . . . it remains true that all who have been justified by faith in baptism are incorporated into Christ . . . Moreover, some, even very many, of the most significant elements and endowments which together go to build up and give life to the Church itself can exist outside the visible boundaries of the Catholic Church . . . All these come from Christ and lead back to him . . . The brethren divided from us also carry out many liturgical actions of the Christian religion . . . these liturgical actions most certainly can truly engender a life of grace and, one must say, can aptly give access to the communion of salvation . . . by no means deprived of significance and importance in the mystery of salvation. For the Spirit of Christ has not refrained from using them as means of salvation . . .[19]

Even as the Catholic Church maintains that the fullness of salvation subsists in the Catholic Church it nonetheless also recognizes that other churches have also been utilized by the Spirit as means of salvation (See *Unitatis Redintegratio*, section 3). With profound humility the Catholic

---

16. Cardman, "One Treasure Only," 174; Rush, *The Vision of Vatican II*, 174, 374.

17. Cardman, "One Treasure Only," 176–7; Rush, *The Vision of Vatican II* 176–177.

18. *Unitatis Redintegratio*, sec. 1.

19. *Unitatis Redintegratio*, sec. 3.

Church also acknowledges that there are times when its own deficiencies in moral conduct and ecclesial teachings and disciplines harm the cause of unity (See *Unitatis Redintegratio*, sections 4, 5, and 7). The Catholic Church also asks forgiveness for its sins against unity (See *Unitatis Redintegratio*, section 7). Such growth marks a departure from the tendency of the Catholic Church to equate itself exclusively with the church of Christ. Ecclesial triumphalism has given way to an openness towards others and a desire for solidarity with other Christians, people of other faiths, and people of good will. Additionally, while the Catholic Church will insist that it possesses the fullness of the means of salvation, it also acknowledges that it is a pilgrim church still growing in Christ and in need of perennial reform, purification, and renewal as it advances toward the "plenitude of truth" (See *Unitatis Redintegratio*, section 6 and *Lumen Gentium*, section 8).

Thanks to the pioneering work of the likes of Yves Congar, OP, and Karl Rahner, SJ, the Catholic Church came to acknowledge anew the universal salvific will of God (See *Lumen Gentium*, sections 9, 14–16, 31 and *Ad Gentes Divinitus*, sections 1–11), the inexhaustibility of revelation (See *Dei Verbum*, sections 2–6, *Unitatis Redintegratio*, section 3, and *Nostra Aetate*, section 2), and the indwelling of the divine in all persons (See *Gaudium et Spes*, section 16 and *Dignitatis Humanae*, section 3). Acknowledgement of the aforesaid implies that God is at work among all people drawing them into relationship. Therefore, particular theologies ought not be confused with the entirety of revelation, rather it should be acknowledged that other religious traditions, like Christianity, contain truth.

In light of this broadening perspective the Second Vatican Council marked a watershed moment in the history of the church vis-à-vis Catholicism's relationship to the other religions of the world. Although it had been anticipated that the church's relationship to Judaism would be addressed by the Council,[20] the Council's consideration of the other world religions was a product of the Council itself as the understanding of God's providence and universal salvific will for all persons emerged from the broader theological framework of the Council which emphasized the Triune God active in the world and the role of the Holy Spirit in the economy of salvation.[21] Additionally, the Council articulated a vision of truth which allows for diverse and pluralistic expressions; the universal scope of revelation; and

---

20. Rush, *Vision of Vatican II*, 426–9, 125–8; Cassidy, *Rediscovering Vatican II*, 125–128.

21. Rush, *Vision of Vatican II*, 426–9, 472.

the innate dignity of all persons endowed with the indwelling of the Spirit and conscience. Each and all of these recognitions underpin the Council's ecumenical and interreligious teachings as does the church's own self-understanding. The church is understood to be missionary by nature sent out to all people to perpetuate Jesus' invitation to all to be in relationship with God. The church is to be a servant on pilgrimage amidst all people acting as a sacrament pointing to and making God present to all. Thus, one must consider Vatican II's ecumenical and interreligious teachings within the context of all the conciliar documents and teachings.[22]

Vatican II's *Pastoral Constitution on the Church in the Modern World* (*Gaudium et Spes*), maintains that the source of all religious experiences is the experience of God. This experience is accessible to all persons and develops within history and in the course of its development takes on a multitude of forms. The awakening of religious awareness is developed in countless stages and in an immense variety of forms. Each stage represents growth in the path toward salvation. The Council's *Declaration on the Church's Relationship to Non-Christian Religions* (*Nostra Aetate*), states:

> Throughout history even to the present day, there is found among different peoples a certain awareness of a hidden power, which lies behind the course of nature and the events of human life . . . This awareness and recognition results in a way of life that is imbued with a deep religious sense . . . The Catholic Church rejects nothing of what is true and holy in these religions. She has a high regard for the manner of life and conduct, precepts and doctrines which . . . reflect a ray of that truth which enlightens all of humanity . . . The Church urges her members to enter with prudence and charity into discussion and collaboration with members of other religions.[23]

It follows that religious experiences are ordered to divine revelation and that natural knowledge of God and supernatural elements of grace are already operative within them for it is presupposed that God wills the

---

22. Rush, *Vision of Vatican II*, 470. As we will see, the Council's Decree on Ecumenism (*Unitatis Redintegratio*) and Declaration on the Church's Relationship to Other Religions (*Nostra Aetate*) must be viewed in relationship with the Council's Dogmatic Constitution on the Church (*Lumen Gentium*), Declaration on Human Dignity (*Dignitatis Humanae*), Decree on Missionary Activity (*Ad Gentes Divinitus*), Dogmatic Constitution on Divine Revelation (*Dei Verbum*), and Pastoral Constitution on the Church in the Modern World (*Gaudium et Spes*).

23. *Nostra Aetate*, sec. 2.

salvation of all persons. As the Council's *Decree on Missionary Activity* (*Ad Gentes*) asserts, "God wishes all persons to be saved and to come to knowledge of the Truth . . . (*Ad Gentes*, section 7)." Hence, when Christianity confronts an adherent of a non-Christian religion it is confronting a person in whom grace is already at work.

In matters pertinent to Christianity the Catholic Church even came to acknowledge that at times truths of the tradition might be better preserved in Christian traditions other than itself. According to *Unitatis Redintegratio*, "It is hardly surprising, then, if sometimes on tradition has come nearer to a full appreciation of some aspects of a mystery of revelation than the other, or has expressed them better."[24]

Furthermore, among such truths there exists a hierarchy. Some truths bear more directly upon Christian soteriology than others. "When comparing doctrines with one another, they should remember that in Catholic doctrine there exists an order or hierarchy of truths, since they vary in their relation to the foundation of the Christian faith," as stated in *Unitatis Redintegratio*.[25]

Hence, in ecumenical and interreligious dialogue no truths beyond that which are necessary should be unduly imposed on others. There can be unity in faith which allows for diversity and plurality of expression. Unity need not require uniformity. Diverse and pluralistic expressions of the truth serve to edify and enhance our understanding of it, not undermine it.

Vatican II and the Theological Nature of Unity and Truth

The directives of the Second Vatican Council maintain that the church, as a pilgrim church, must embrace the fact that the church and theology are subject to the historical demands and conditions of the times in which they find themselves. The church must adapt and modify itself and its theology accordingly to be as effective as possible in its mission (See *Lumen Gentium*, section 48 and *Gaudium et Spes* sections 39, 40, and 57). Given the vast diversity of cultures which mark the lived experiences of all peoples, the church will have to be open to inculturation and to appreciating (as

---

24. *Unitatis Redintegratio*, sec. 17.
25. *Unitatis Redintegratio*, sec. 11.

did the churches of the apostolic period[26]) unity in the midst of diversity. Again, unity need not, and does not, equal uniformity.

The theological question becomes one regarding the nature of truth. How is truth best ascertained and communicated? Via a single, uniform expression? Or via diverse and pluralistic expressions? The Christian tradition has always recognized that the truth can be preserved and communicated via diverse and pluralistic means. Indeed, one can say that the apostolicity of the church, which serves its catholicity, requires that the church be open to diverse and pluralistic expressions of faith.

The Christian understanding of God as a Triune God accentuates the Christian conviction that truth expresses itself in diverse and pluralistic ways. Such expression does not compromise the truth, but rather provides a greater understanding of the truth. Each person of the Trinity is a unique expression of the same truth (divine nature), yet each person in their unique personhood and unique role in the economy of salvation expresses this selfsame truth in a unique manner. Our understanding of the divine is not compromised as a result of these diverse and pluralistic expressions, rather our understanding of the divine is enhanced because of them.

The Christian tradition has come to accept four diverse and pluralistic accounts of God's saving action in the person of Jesus: the gospels of Matthew, Mark, Luke, and John. Each of the gospels convey the selfsame truth regarding salvation from God through Jesus, yet each gospel communicates this selfsame truth in its own unique way. Each of the unique expressions regarding Jesus proffered in the gospels reflects the culture, climate, and conditions of the community which proffered it. Again, our understanding of God's saving action in Jesus is not compromised because of the richly diverse and pluralistic expressions of the four gospels, rather our understanding of Jesus is enhanced. Just think how impoverished our understanding of Jesus would be if we only had one of the gospels . . . Or if we had four gospels which were exactly the same. Without John's gospel we would know nothing of Jesus' pre-existence as the Word of God through whom God created the universe, and we would know nothing of the raising of Lazarus. Without Matthew's and Luke's gospels we would know nothing of Jesus' birth and infancy. Without Luke we would lack the seminal parables of the Prodigal Son and Good Samaritan . . . etc.

---

26. For additional reading on the apostolicity of the church, see Burkhard, *Apostolicity Then and Now.*

The early faith communities of Christianity did not feel compelled to hold a single uniform expression of the faith but, rather, embraced their diverse lived experiences and expressions as faithful witnesses to God's saving designs through the person of Jesus. Diverse and pluralistic expressions of the truth serve to edify and enhance our understanding of it, not undermine it.

Also consider the apostolic witness of ecclesial toleration. St. Paul consistently makes clear that the early church tolerated diverse and pluralistic ecclesial expressions and practices while understanding themselves united under a single head, Jesus. Paul's favored image for the church is the body of Christ. With Christ as the head of the body each church community (member even) represents a part of the body with its unique contribution to the whole. The body functions precisely because of the diverse and pluralistic parts it has, each working together to enhance the overall experience of the whole. To function properly a body needs its various members performing their various tasks. A body comprised of a single part or faculty would not be viable. The New Testament also reveals that the early church communities tolerated diverse and pluralistic expressions for the sake of unity in the body under the head—Christ—with such episodes as the Jerusalem Conference (circumcised and uncircumcised were welcomed) and the episode between Peter and Cornelius (Jew and Gentile were welcomed), etc. (See Acts 15 and 10).

We in the contemporary church need to recognize the inexhaustible means by which God reveals truth and follow the example of the New Testament and apostolic communities of faith. We need to share our experience of God and understanding of truth with others while also being humbly open to and receptive of what others share of God's self-disclosure and communication of truth as they experience and understand them. Doing so broadens our understanding of and relationship with God (vertical communion) while also enhancing our relationships with others (horizontal communion). An ecumenical openness to the diverse and pluralistic expressions of truth helps us all to come to better understand and know God and one another. As Pope Francis noted, "An attitude of openness in truth and in love must characterize the dialogue with the followers of non-Christian religions . . . Interreligious dialogue is a necessary condition for peace in the world, and so it is a duty for Christians as well as other religious communities."[27]

27. *Evangelium Gaudium*, sec. 250.

Dei Verbum: Vatican II on Divine Revelation

The scope of revelation is universal. . . . "God our savior . . . wants all people to be saved and come to know the truth" (1 Timothy 2:4). God reveals God-self to all for all share the common destiny of union with God. The Holy Spirit illuminates said revelation. It follows, therefore, that the causes of ecumenism and interreligious dialogue require that one be open to what God is making known to others and that one recognize the Spirit working within the lives of every person. God reveals Godself to every human being and invites every human being into friendship. If God desires friendship with others, ought not we?

> In His goodness and wisdom God chose to reveal Himself and to make known to us the hidden purpose of His will (see Ephesians 1:9) by which through Christ, the Word made flesh, people might in the Holy Spirit have access to the Father and come to share in the divine nature (see Eph. 2:18; 2 Peter 1:4). Through this revelation, therefore, the invisible God (see Colossians 1;15, 1 Timothy 1:17) out of the abundance of His love speaks to people as friends (see Exodus 33:11; John 15:14–15) and lives among them (see Baruch 3:38), so that He may invite and take them into fellowship with Himself. This plan of revelation is realized by deeds and words having an inner unity: the deeds wrought by God in the history of salvation manifest and confirm the teaching and realities signified by the words, while the words proclaim the deeds and clarify the mystery contained in them. By this revelation then, the deepest truth about God and the salvation of people shines out . . . [28]

The words and deeds of others bear vestiges of God. Hence, we can come to know and understand God more fully if we respectfully observe and learn from others.

> To make this act of faith, the grace of God and the interior help of the Holy Spirit must precede and assist, moving the heart and turning it to God, opening the eyes of the mind and giving "joy and ease to everyone in assenting to the truth and believing it."
>
> To bring about an ever deeper understanding of revelation the same Holy Spirit constantly brings faith to completion by His gifts. Through divine revelation, God chose to show forth and communicate Himself and the eternal decisions of His will regarding the salvation of all. That is to say, He chose to share with them

---

28. *Dei Verbum*, sec. 2.

those divine treasures which totally transcend the understanding of the human mind. As a sacred synod has affirmed, God, the beginning and end of all things, can be known with certainty from created reality by the light of human reason (see Romans 1:20); but teaches that it is through His revelation that those religious truths which are by their nature accessible to human reason can be known by all . . . [29]

The Holy Spirit is active in the lives of all aiding their comprehension of God so that all may know God's will and be in relationship with God. Where the Spirit is active there is grace. Grace is active in the lives of all human beings. Therefore, when we encounter others we are afforded grace. Vatican II moved the church beyond its traditional propositional understanding of revelation to an understanding of revelation as an inter-personal communication initiated by God with each/all persons animated and guided by the Spirit who illumines the relationship. The Council opened the church to God's/the Spirit's action in the lives of others and, therefore, to ecumenical and interreligious efforts.

DIGNITATIS HUMANAE: VATICAN II ON HUMAN DIGNITY

One cannot appreciate the Second Vatican Council's radical commitment to ecumenism and interreligious dialogue without also appreciating the Council's wider anthropology, particularly the Council's affirmation of religious freedom as the constitutive hallmark of human dignity, i.e., human beings being created in the image and likeness of God.[30] Human beings are free and endowed by God with conscience whereby God addresses each individual deep within oneself. God invites every person to do what is right and to shun that which is wrong. Every person is invited by God to be in relationship with God. Nothing is to impede, manipulate, or coerce the individual's response to this divine invitation. In matters of religion freedom of conscience is sacrosanct and inviolate.

The Vatican Council declares that the human person has a right to religious freedom. Freedom of this kind means that all persons should be immune from coercion on the part of individuals, social groups, and every human power so that nobody is forced to

29. *Dei Verbum*, secs. 5–6.

30. Rush, *Vision of Vatican II*, 470, 476; *Gaudium et Spes*, secs. 12, 22, 24, 26, 29, 34, 41, 52, 68.

act against their convictions in religious matters . . . The Council further declares that the right to religious freedom is based in the very dignity of the human person . . . It is through one's conscience that one sees and recognizes the demands of the divine law. One is bound to follow this conscience faithfully in all of their activity so that they may come to God, who is their last end. Therefore, one must not be forced to act contrary to their conscience. Nor must one be prevented from acting in accord with one's conscience, especially in religious matters . . . to deny one the free exercise of religion . . . is to do an injustice to the human person and to the very order established by God . . . [31]

The Council reaffirmed the witness of scripture and the church fathers which teach that human responses to God/acts of faith must be free. Prior to the Second Vatican Council it had been long maintained by the Catholic Church that states had the obligation to ensure the practice of Catholicism and to impede the practice of other faiths for it was maintained that error had no rights, and other religions were deemed erroneous. Indeed, as late as 1864, Pope Pius IX, in his *Syllabus of Errors*, and Pope Pius X, in his 1907 encyclical *Pascendi Domenici Gregis*, rejected the notion of religious freedom. Such a stance became increasingly problematic in the wake of the Protestant Reformation (whereby efforts towards peace resulted in the faith of the prince being the faith of a region); the English Reformation (whereby the king of England asserted his authority over the church in England); and the emerging democracies subsequent to the French and American Revolutions. Nonetheless, those within the Catholic Church, like John Courtney Murray, SJ, who espoused religious freedom, were silenced and removed from their teaching positions in the years just prior to the Second Vatican Council . . . only to be vindicated by the teachings of the Council itself.[32] It is worth considering that many of the courageous pioneers of ecumenism and interreligious dialogue within Roman Catholicism such as Karl Rahner, SJ, and Yves Congar, OP, suffered greatly for their views. Many were silenced, stripped of their priesthood, forbidden to publish and teach . . . only to be vindicated at the Council as many of these same persons would serve as theological advisors and draft various Council documents. One must be cautious with labels such as heretic/liberal, for one decade's heretic/liberal might be the next decade's architect/voice of orthodoxy.

31. *Dignitatis Humanae*, secs. 2, 3, 10; *Gaudium et Spes*, sec.16.

32. For an overview of the development of religious freedom, see Bevans and Gros, *Rediscovering Vatican II*, 151.

With this anthropological understanding whereby it is recognized that God speaks to every individual directly, the Council yet again acknowledges that God and God's efforts to make Godself known are operative within every individual. Therefore, every individual has the potential to disclose something of God to us. We ought to be open to and receptive of what an encounter with another might reveal to us about God. Hence, the Council's teaching regarding human dignity, conscience, and religious freedom are yet additional catalysts for committing oneself to ecumenical and interreligious efforts. Said anthropological understanding is also a caution against any type of religious imperialism which would impede one from acting according to one's conscience or be forced to act against it in matters of religion. Ecclesial and/or theological attempts to do so would be an affront to the dignity of the human person and to God. What we Christians claim about the human person necessitates that we be respectful of and open to what God is doing within every individual facilitating their free response in matters of religious belief.

Ad Gentes Divinitus: Vatican II on the Church's Missionary Nature

The Council's accent upon ecumenism and interreligious dialogue must also be viewed in light of the church's self-understanding of its missionary nature. *Ad Gentes* posits that "The pilgrim Church is missionary by her very nature . . . (*Ad Gentes*, section 2)." The church's very essence demands that the church go forth to encounter others. This is how the church faithfully honors the great commission Jesus bestowed upon it. In going forth, however, the church must be mindful of what has been said above: revelation, truth, grace, holiness, God, and the Spirit are already active in the lives of all those whom the church encounters for God wills the salvation of all (See *Ad Gentes Divintus* sections 2–4, 7, and 9).[33]

Hence, missionary efforts are a two-way dialectic whereby the church not only proclaims the redemptive and salvific designs of the Christ Event, but is also open to what God is already doing in the lives of those whom the church encounters. As stated in *Ad-Gentes*, "But whatever truth and grace are to be found among the nations, as a sort of secret presence of God . . . And so, whatever good is found to be sown in the hearts and minds of women and men, or in the rites and cultures peculiar to various peoples,

33. Rush, *Vision of Vatican II*, 474–475.

not only is not lost, but is healed, uplifted, and perfected for the glory of God."[34]

The church not only has something to offer others via missionary efforts, but also stands to gain truth, grace, healing, God's presence, and glory from those who are encountered. Such gifts, like the gospel which the church shares, can be uplifting and lend to the church's own perfection. Therefore, Christians should dialogue with others so that they may learn more of God's generosity (See *Ad Gentes Divinitus* sections 11, 12, 16, 34, and 41).[35] Missionary efforts lend to ecumenical and interreligious dialogue when carried out with humility, deference, and respect for God's presence and actions at work in those encountered. Again, *Ad Gentes* states that: ". . . disciples, profoundly penetrated by the Spirit of Christ, should know the people among whom they live, and should converse with them, that they themselves may learn by sincere and patient dialogue what treasures a generous God has distributed among the nations of the earth."[36]

GAUDIUM ET SPES: VATICAN II'S PASTORAL COMMITMENT TO ALL

Along with the aforesaid discussed *Decree on Missionary Activity*, Vatican II's *Pastoral Constitution on the Church in the Modern World* (*Gaudium et Spes*), mark the Council's two longest promulgated documents. Consider this: the Council's documents considering the church being sent out *ad extra* to the world are its longest. This says much about the Council's understanding of the church and its need to go outside of itself and go forth to others. The church has the gospel to offer those outside of it, but those outside of the church have much to offer the church in return. *Gaudium et Spes* committed the church to pastorally engaging all persons of the world while respecting the myriad of diverse and pluralistic human cultures.

> The joy and hope, the grief and anguish of the people of our time . . . are the joy and hope, the grief and anguish of the followers of Christ as well . . . the Second Vatican Council . . . resolutely addresses . . . the whole of humanity . . . the world which the Council has in mind is the whole human family seen in context

---

34. *Ad Gentes Divinitus*, sec. 9.

35. Rush, *Vision of Vatican II*, 475.

36. *Ad Gentes Divinitus*, sec. 11.

of everything which envelopes it . . . the Spirit of the Lord fills the
whole world . . . [37]

Giving additional voice to the church's anthropological understanding
Gaudium et Spes commits the church to all persons and all cultures for all
human beings have been touched by the Incarnation, i.e., by the fact that
Jesus assumed human nature. Every human being illuminates the mystery
of the Incarnation. Echoing *Dignitatis Humanae*, *Gaudium et Spes* reaffirms
that the human person is created in the image and likeness of God and is
endowed with conscience, again directing one's attention to the indwelling
and action of God present in every human being.

> In the depths of his conscience, one detects a law which one does
> not impose upon oneself, but which holds one to obedience. Al-
> ways summoning one to love good and avoid evil, the voice of
> conscience when necessary speaks to one's heart: do this, shun
> that. For one has in one's heart a law written by God; to obey it
> is the very dignity of the human person; according to it one will
> be judged. Conscience is the most secret core and sanctuary of a
> person. There one is alone with God, whose voice echoes in one's
> depths.[38]

Together with God's workings within every individual, God also pen-
etrates human cultures so as to open up avenues of truth and to shed light
on the destiny of every human being.[39] The Council asserts, "It is one of the
properties of the human person that one can achieve true and full humanity only by means of culture . . ."[40]

As instruments employed by God to reveal truth and illuminate human destiny, cultures share the aims and goals of religion. Cultures, like
religion, help us to know and understand God by providing ways for us to
discover and express truths germane to human existence. Consequently,
the church ought to engage and work with human cultures to advance the
cause of faith.[41] Just as the Council's understandings of truth, revelation,
anthropology, and missiology advance the cause of ecumenical and interreligious dialogue so, too, does the Council's commitment to inculturation.

37. *Gaudium et Spes*, secs. 1, 2, 11.

38. *Gaudium et Spes*, secs.16, 26, 29; Rush, *Vision of Vatican II*, 476.

39. *Gaudium et Spes*, sec. 44.

40. *Gaudium et Spes*, sec. 53.

41. *Gaudium et Spes*, secs. 58, 62.

... God desired that all people should form one family and deal
with each other in a spirit of brotherhood ... for all people of
good will in whose hearts grace works in an unseen way ... Christ
died for all and since the ultimate vocation of a human being is in
fact one, and divine, we ought to believe that the Holy Spirit in a
manner known only to God offers to every person the possibility
of being associated with this paschal mystery.[42]

NOSTRA AETATE: VATICAN II ON THE CHURCH'S RELATIONSHIP WITH NON-CHRISTIAN RELIGIONS

The Second Vatican Council committed the Roman Catholic Church to
dialogue with persons of other religions—and of no religion at all—in an
unprecedented and unparalleled manner. The Council's *Declaration on the
Church's Relationship with Non-Christian Religions (Nostra Aetate)*, points
out that all persons come from the one and same God and share a common
destiny. It recognizes that throughout history there can be found an awareness of a hidden power and recognition of a supreme being which have
given rise to ways of life imbued with a deep religious sense. It proclaims
that the Catholic Church accepts truth and holiness in other religions and
maintains that conversation and collaboration among members of different
religions is necessary.

> Throughout history even to the present day, there is found among
> different peoples a certain awareness of a hidden power, which
> lies behind the course of nature and the events of human life ...
> This awareness and recognition results in a way of life that is im-
> bued with a deep religious sense ... The Catholic Church rejects
> nothing of what is true and holy in these religions. She has a high
> regard for the manner of life and conduct, precepts, and doctrines
> which ... reflect a ray of that truth which enlightens all of human-
> ity ... The Church urges her members to enter with prudence and
> charity into discussion and collaboration with members of other
> religions.[43]

How can one who desires to understand and know God not be open
to God's presence, truth, and holiness to be discovered in the religious traditions of the world? No one religious tradition can exhaust the mystery

---

42. *Gaudium et Spes*, secs. 22, 24, 12, 29, 34, 41, 52, 68.
43. *Nostra Aetate*, sec. 2.

of God, completely and perfectly convey truth, nor monopolize holiness. Likewise, no one religion has a corner on depravity and falsehood.

> We cannot truly pray to God the Father of all if we treat any people as other than sisters and brothers, for all are created in God's image. People's relation to God the Father and their relation to other women and men are so dependent on each other that the Scripture says, "They who do not love, do not know God" (1 John 4:8).[44]

If we visualize God as the sun and the multiplicity of religions as recipients of various rays of the sun, if we wish to have the most comprehensive understanding of God, receive the most rays of the sun, must we not be open to others who receive rays shone upon them that differ from the rays shone upon us? As Pope Francis has said:

> If we really believe in the abundantly free working of the Holy Spirit, we can learn so much from one another! It is not just about being better informed about others, but rather about reaping what the Spirit has sown in them, which is also meant to be a gift for us.[45]
>
> Non-Christians, by God's gracious initiative, when they are faithful to their own consciences, can live "justified by the grace of God," and thus be "associated to the Paschal mystery of Jesus Christ" ... God's working in them tends to produce signs and rites, sacred expressions which in turn bring others to a communitarian experience of journeying towards God ... they can be channels which the Holy Spirit raises up ... The same Spirit everywhere brings forth various forms of practical wisdom which help people to bear suffering and to live in greater peace and harmony. As Christians, we can also benefit from these treasures built up over many centuries, which can help us better to live our own beliefs.[46]

In light of our contemporary sensitivities to other persons born out of the efforts of ecumenism and interreligious dialogue, as well as the increasing globalization[47] of the world, Christianity has to address the question of how it relates to all persons—persons of other faiths as well as non-believers. The challenge for Christians lies in tempering rigid Christo-centrism (the

44. *Nostra Aetate*, sec. 5.

45. Francis, *Evangelii Gaudium*, sec. 246.

46. Francis, *Evangelii Gaudium*, sec. 254.

47. Globalization refers to the growing interactions, interconnectedness, and interdependence among the world's cultures and peoples.

insistence upon the requisite necessity of Jesus for salvation) to be open to God's saving designs in other religions of the world, while avoiding a kind of relativism which would compromise the unsurpassable saving designs of God offered through the Christ Event. As Christians we must come to understand that our fidelity to Christianity need not mean that we separate ourselves from others, nor deny God's working among others.

Commitment to our own faith need not lead us to denigrate the faith of others, nor preclude us from being open to God's work within them.[48] At issue, it seems, is the apparent tension within the Christian tradition which posits that every person is created in the image and likeness of God (indwelt by the Spirit and endowed with conscience) and destined for union with God vis-à-vis the claim that Jesus Christ is the mediator of God's grace necessary unto salvation. Additional tensions flow from the Catholic recognition of truth, goodness, and holiness (God and the Spirit's work) operative in other religions of the world vis-à-vis its claims about Jesus. How is it then that Christianity can affirm all these claims?

Obviously, many Christians don't. Some maintain that only if one comes to an explicit affirmation and acceptance of Jesus as one's savior can one be saved. This stance is frequently referred to as a constitutive exclusive stance. Jesus is so constitutively necessary for salvation that all other means devoid of Christ are excluded from the possibility of salvation. Others maintain that Jesus is not constitutive for salvation but provides a normative example. This stance maintains that the saving grace of God is not exhausted by one saving figure or plan of salvation but incorporates a plethora of different salvific figures and plans of salvation. Jesus is helpful in that he, along with other saving figures, illuminates God's will and what is necessary for us to experience God's saving grace. We will call this stance the normative stance. Others maintain that Jesus is necessary for salvation but that this can be understood in an inclusive sense, i.e., that Jesus—understood by Christians to be truth, goodness, and holiness—is operative in some fashion in any religion in which truth, goodness, and holiness are found. Hence this stance is termed a constitutive inclusive stance. Here the focus is on God's universal salvific will and how that comes into focus in the person of Jesus who died to save all persons. Recognized as the source of all truth, goodness, and grace, Christ is seen as constitutively necessary for salvation. However, it is also recognized that when truth, goodness, and grace can be found and are operative outside of Christianity these, too,

---

48. Rush, *Vision of Vatican II*, 479.

are sufficient unto salvation for they are derived from the same and only source, namely Jesus.

Consequently, whenever one responds to the truth, goodness, and grace, one is implicitly, if not explicitly, responding to Christ. Hence Christ can be said to be constitutively necessary for salvation but in a way that includes religions devoid of explicit claims regarding Christ. This position is also known as inclusive pluralism. It safeguards the uniqueness of the Christ Event for salvation while at the same time recognizing the possibility of salvation in other religions for their followers. This is the position articulated in the comprehensive teachings of the Second Vatican Council.[49]

It is helpful to recall as well that a striking feature of the first century Christian community was the acute awareness that there was something still outstanding in their experience of the life, death, and resurrection of Jesus. This unfinished and incomplete eschatological work of Jesus is expressed in a variety of ways but consistently in the earliest christologies of the New Testament. Christianity remained an open narrative. Perhaps by being open to ecumenism and interreligious dialogue the narrative can continue to be written as we await the full disclosure of God's saving designs upon the end times. The incredible advances that have been made in Catholic-Jewish relations since the Council can serve as an example of what can be accomplished in interreligious dialogue.[50] As illustrative, the church has come to affirm Judaism as its parent religion from whom Jesus, Mary, the disciples, Paul, the earliest Christians, scriptures, and sacraments came. The church acknowledges a single covenant of redemption shared by Jews and Christians and that Judaism's share in the covenant has never been revoked for God is faithful to God's promises. Accusations of deicide against Jews have been abandoned by the church as have theologies of contempt which suggested that Christianity had usurped and superseded Judaism. All forms of antisemitism have been condemned by the church and all efforts of proselytizing Jews forbidden.

---

49. *Nostra Aetate* seemingly espouses a constitutive inclusive position and the wider Conciliar documents echo early patristic notions which deem truth, goodness, and holiness operative among those lacking an explicit faith in Christ as preparation for the gospel (e.g., Eusebius of Caesarea) and/or recognizes the aforesaid as seeds of the Word/Jesus (e.g., Justin Martyr) sown among all peoples out of God's providence, revelation, and universal saving designs; Rush, *Vision of Vatican II*, 473.

50. For a sense of the multitude of advances in Catholic-Jewish dialogue in the decades subsequent to the Second Vatican Council, see the Vatican's Commission for Religious Relations; Cassidy, *Rediscovering Vatican II*, 241–63.

Unitatis Redintegratio: Vatican II on the Church's Relationship to Other Christians

It only makes sense that if the church's fidelity to the universal salvific mission of Jesus, which constitutes the very essence and nature of the church, unto all religions, cultures, and peoples of the world is to be credible and efficacious, then a commitment to the restoration of unity among Christians must be a prerequisite to wider efforts of unity. Such restoration of unity with other Christians is the focus of the Second Vatican Council's *Decree on Ecumenism (Unitatis Redintegratio)*. The document situates the Catholic approach to ecumenism within the context of Christ's prayer for the church, the Holy Spirit's activity within the church, and the exemplary model of communion revealed to us via the Trinity and maintains that:

> The restoration of unity among all Christians is one of the principal concerns of the Second Vatican Council . . . division openly contradicts the will of Christ, scandalizes the world, and damages the most holy cause, the preaching of the Gospel to every creature (*Unitatis Redintegratio*, section 1).
>
> It is the Council's urgent desire that every effort should be made toward the gradual realization of this unity (*Unitatis Redintegratio*, section 18).

As noted above, toward the goal of Christian unity the Catholic Church humbly voiced in the decree an admission of guilt on the part of the Roman Church for historical Christian divisions and recognized that other traditions have at times better expressed the truths of revelation (See *Unitatis Redintegratio*, sections 3, 7, 17):

> . . . sometimes one tradition has come nearer to a full appreciation of some aspects of a mystery of revelation than the other, or has expressed them better."[51]

Furthermore, a description of Orthodox and Protestant churches was articulated which deemed said churches to be "churches and ecclesial communities" endowed with the charisms of salvation and the primacy of Baptism (See *Unitatis Redintegratio*, sections 3, 21, 22, 23).[52]

> . . . all who have been justified by faith in baptism are incorporated into Christ . . . many of the most significant elements and

---

51. *Unitatis Redintegratio*, sec.17.

52. Rush, *Vision of Vatican II*, 388–407.

endowments which together go to build up and give life to the
Church can exist outside the . . . Catholic Church . . . The brethren divided from us also carry out many liturgical actions of the
Christian religion . . . these liturgical actions most certainly can
truly engender a life of grace and . . . can aptly give access to the
communion of salvation . . . It follows that the separated Churches
and communities . . . have been by no means deprived of significance and importance in the mystery of salvation. For the Spirit
of Christ has not refrained from using them as means of salvation
(*Unitatis Redintegratio*, section 3).

Here the Catholic Church explicitly acknowledges the elements which
constitute an authentic church exist within non-Catholic faith communities and that the liturgical actions of non-Catholic Christian communities
engender grace and afford access to salvation for the Holy Spirit is operative
within them. Again, as noted above, the decree also spoke of a hierarchy of
truths in regard to Christian teachings noting that some aspects of the faith
bear more directly upon the Christian understanding of salvation than
others:

> When comparing doctrines with one another they should remem-
> ber that in Catholic doctrine there exists a hierarchy of truths,
> since they vary in their relation to the foundation of the Christian
> faith."[53]

Therefore, when striving for unity no burden beyond that which is
necessary should be unduly imposed upon another. While engaging in ecumenical dialogue we need to be open to a conversion of heart and mind as
we allow that the Holy Spirit informs doctrines, disciplines, and practices
different from our own.[54]

> Nor should we forget that anything wrought by the grace of the
> Holy Spirit in the hearts of our separated brothers and sisters can
> contribute to our own edification. Whatever is truly Christian is
> never contrary to what genuinely belongs to the faith; indeed it
> can always bring a more perfect realization of the very mystery of
> Christ and the church.[55]

The decades after the Second Vatican Council have seen tremendous
strides in the cause of ecumenism. Dialogue and collaboration among the

---

53. *Unitatis Redintegratio*, sec.11; Rush, *Vision of Vatican II*, 422.

54. Rush, *Vision of Vatican II*, 420.

55. *Unitatis Redintegratio*, sec. 4.

array of Christian traditions has occurred and yielded much fruit.[56] However, remaining disparate views regarding ecclesial hierarchy, holy orders, and the Eucharist, particularly, continue to impede Christian unity.[57]

Roman Catholicism maintains that authentic episcopal apostolic succession requires union with the papacy. Hence, even those Protestant traditions which are episcopally structured but not in union with the papacy are deemed to lack apostolic succession.

Additionally, Roman Catholicism maintains that holy orders (ordination to the priesthood) is a sacrament which can only be conferred by a bishop in apostolic succession and that the sacrament effects an ontological change (a change in one's being and essence via an indelible mark upon one's soul, also known as sacramental character) in the recipient enabling them to act in the person of Jesus on behalf of the church. Protestant orders, therefore, are deemed to be invalid for they are not conferred by a bishop in apostolic succession and they are not understood to effect an ontological change in the recipient.[58] Rather, Protestant understandings of ordination tend to differentiate the ordained functionally from others within the faith community given their particular service of the word within the life of the faith community. Also, many Protestant traditions allow for the ordination of women whereas, as we saw in the first chapter, Roman Catholicism ordains only men.

Lastly, Roman Catholicism understands the Eucharist to be the real presence of Jesus—Jesus substantively present in body, mind, soul, and divinity via the miracle of transubstantiation. Transubstantiation involves a miracle whereby there is an inversion of the natural order. In the order of nature, substances (the essence/nature of things) remain the same while accidents (mutable appearances under which substances exist) change. Via transubstantiation the substance of bread and wine changes into the body and blood of Jesus while the accidents of bread and wine remain the same. While some Protestant understandings of the Eucharist maintain

---

56. For a sense of the tremendous ecumenical advances between the Catholic Church and other Christian traditions since the Second Vatican Council see the Pontifical Council for the Promotion of Christian Unity. As illustrative, one can see Catholic-Lutheran Dialogue, *From Conflict to Communion*.

57. US Catholic Bishop's Committee on Ecumenical and Interreligious Affairs and the ELCA, *Declaration on the Way*, 15, 55.

58. US Catholic Bishop's Committee on Ecumenical and Interreligious Affairs and ELCA, *Declaration on the Way*, 15, 55.

real presence,[59] they do not appeal to transubstantiation as a definitively exhaustive explanation for how this comes about. Roman Catholicism has absolutized transubstantiation as the only definitive, exhaustive, and acceptable explanation for real presence thereby making belief in transubstantiation as requisite for intercommunion with other Christians rather than real presence per se.[60] This is problematic in my judgment for it gives the impression that that which is ultimately a miracle and mystery (which are by their very nature beyond definitive and exhaustive explanation) can be definitively and exhaustively explained. It also fails to do justice to other factors which also lend to real presence such as the gathered assembly, the corporate act of *anamnesis* (communal act of remembrance), *epiclesis* (prayer calling down the Holy Spirit to effect the change), and recitation of the words of institution ("Do this in remembrance of me").

Although there have been strides made in the ecumenical movement vis-à-vis recognition of the promise and potential of the papacy as a symbol of Christian unity there obviously remain disparate views among Christians regarding the nature of papal authority in ecclesial governance and the requisite need for bishops to be united to the papacy if to be said to be in apostolic succession.[61] The challenge for Catholics is one of recognizing legitimate apostolic succession among bishops not in full communion with papacy for this not only informs the Catholic notion of apostolic succession but the validity of Protestant orders within traditions which have bishops.

Can Catholicism understand holy orders and the priesthood in a way that does not insist upon an ontological distinction between the ordained and other members of the faith community? Can service, charisms, and communal deputation be viewed as sufficient for differentiating the ordained from the laity?

Lastly, can Catholicism, for the sake of Christian Eucharistic unity, allow for alternative explications of how real presence is brought about? Is it not hubris to suggest that there is only one definitive and exhaustive way to explain that which is ultimately a miracle and mystery? Can transubstantiation be one acceptable way among many of understanding the miracle of Eucharistic real presence? Especially since the concept itself is

59. US Catholic Bishop's Committee on Ecumenical and Interreligious Affairs and ELCA, *Declaration on the Way*, 15, 55.

60. Schillebeeckx was admonished by Rome for his articulation of the Eucharistic mystery of real presence in terms of transignification.

61. Anglican-Roman Catholic International Commission, *Authority in Church 2*, 32–33; Bishops of the Church of England, *May They All Be One*, 19–20.

a development which comes to be articulated a millennium into the development of the Christian tradition. As a Jew celebrating the Passover/ Last Supper would not *anamnesis* be more true to Jesus' and the disciples' understanding of real presence?

LUMEN GENTIUM: VATICAN II'S ECCLESIAL SELF-UNDERSTANDING

The conciliar teachings illuminate a new ecclesial self-awareness within Roman Catholicism which acknowledges that the church is a pilgrim church (See *Lumen Gentium*, Chapter 7) called to pastorally engage and serve all people if it is to be true to the mandate/commission bestowed upon it by Jesus (See *Gaudium et Spes* and *Ad Gentes Divinitus*). The church must go forth to all to serve as a sacrament pointing to and making present the love of God to all (See *Ad Gentes Divinitus*, section 1; *Lumen Gentium*, sections 9, 11, 48; and *Gaudium et Spes*, section 45). Fidelity to the universal saving designs of God demands that the church be committed to ecumenism and interreligious dialogue. All people are related to the church and called to be people of God (See *Lumen Gentium*, sections 16 and 13).[62] All human beings are children of God sharing a common human nature and a common destiny. The catholicity of the church requires that the church work for unity among all people.[63] Vis-à-vis other Christians the Council recognized other Christians as being members of churches and/or ecclesial communities in varying degrees of communion with the Catholic Church.[64]

After Vatican II Pope John Paul II dedicated one of his longest encyclicals, *Ut Unum Sint*, to the cause of ecumenism for he believed that ecumenical unity was the prayer and will of Jesus for the church. The pope matter-of-factly asserted: ". . . believers in Christ . . . cannot remain divided . . . the unity of all divided humankind is the will of God . . ."[65] He invited all Christians to join him in recognizing their mistakes and sins against unity (See *Ut Unum Sint* sections 2–3); to examine one's conscience and repent for these mistakes and sins (See *Ut Unum Sint* sections 34 and 15); and to be open to unity unto diversity (See *Ut Unum Sint* sections 19, 54, and 60).

---

62. Rush, *Vision of Vatican II*, 471.

63. Rush, *Vision of Vatican II*, 47; *Lumen Gentium*, sec. 13

64. Rush, *Vision of Vatican II*, 400–15; *Lumen Gentium*, sec. 15; *Unitatis Redintegratio*, sec. 3.

65. John Paul II, *Ut Unum Sint*, secs. 1, 6.

The pope asserted that, "The Second Vatican Council made it clear that elements present among other Christians can contribute to the edification of Catholics; Nor should we forget that whatever is wrought by the Holy Spirit in the hearts of our separated brethren can contribute to our own edification."[66]

When is the time for ecumenical unity? Now, for the Second Vatican Council did irrevocably commit the Catholic Church to ecumenism and interreligious dialogue: "At all times and in every race, anyone who fears God and does what is right has been acceptable to Him."[67]

> All people are called to belong to the People of God. This People, therefore, whilst remaining one and only one, is to be spread throughout the whole world and to all ages in order that the designs of God's will may be fulfilled: He made human nature one in the beginning and has decreed that all His children who are scattered should finally be gathered together as one . . . All the faithful scattered throughout the world are in communion with one another in the Holy Spirit . . . In virtue of this catholicity each part contributes its own gifts to other parts . . . so that the whole and each of its parts are strengthened by the common sharing and by the common effort to attain the fullness of unity.[68]
>
> . . . Christians are indeed in some real way joined with us in the Holy Spirit for by his gifts and graces his sanctifying power is also active in them . . . [69]
>
> But the plan of salvation also includes those who acknowledge the Creator. Nor is God far distant from those who in shadows and images seek the unknown God, for it is He who gives to all people life and breath and all things, and as Savior wills that all be saved. Those also can attain to salvation who through no fault of their own do not know the Gospel of Christ or His Church, yet sincerely seek God and moved by grace strive by their deeds to do His will as it is known to them through the dictates of conscience. Nor does Divine Providence deny the helps necessary for salvation to those who, without blame on their part, have not yet arrived at an explicit knowledge of God and with His grace strive to live a good life. Whatever good or truth is found amongst them is looked upon by the Church as a preparation for the Gospel.[70]

66. John Paul II, *Ut Unum Sint*, sec. 48.

67. *Lumen Gentium*, sec. 9.

68. *Lumen Gentium*, sec. 13.

69. *Lumen Gentium*, sec. 15.

70. *Lumen Gentium*, sec. 16.

Regarding relationships among Christians we must strive to further understand Catholic claims that the fullness of salvation subsists in the Catholic Church while also acknowledging the Spirit's utilization of other Christian traditions also endowed with sanctifying grace and which are vehicles of salvation in their own right. Regarding persons of non-Christian religions we must strive to further understand how the Spirit indwells within every person and shines forth rays of truth, goodness, and holiness within these religious traditions. We must strive to understand how the Spirit imbues them with a deep religious and spiritual sense which produces a moral life and lends to the perfection of its practitioners. It is the Spirit who endows all traditions with grace. It is the Spirit who God employs to draw all persons to Godself. It is the Spirit who orients all towards God. Hence, pneumatology (an appreciation for the working of the Spirit) is indispensable to ecumenism and inter-religious dialogue. Perhaps not coincidentally this is why Pope John XXIII consistently referred to the Second Vatican Council as a new Pentecost. And why Yves Congar, OP, deemed the life of the Church to be one long *epiclesis*.[71]

> We need to go further back, to embrace the whole of the action of the Holy Spirit even . . . from the beginning, throughout the world . . . For this action has been exercised, in every place and at every time, indeed in every individual, according to the eternal plan of salvation . . . Grace, therefore, bears within itself both a pneumatological aspect . . . The Second Vatican Council, centered primarily on the theme of the Church, reminds us of the Holy Spirit's activity also "outside the visible body of the Church." The council speaks precisely of "all people of good will in whose hearts grace works in an unseen way. For, since Christ died for all, and since the ultimate vocation of man is in fact one, and divine, we ought to believe that the Holy Spirit in a manner known only to God offers to every person the possibility of being associated with this Paschal Mystery"[72]
>
> The Spirit manifests Himself in a special way in the Church and in her members. Nevertheless, his presence and activity are universal, limited neither by space nor time. The Second Vatican Council recalls that the Spirit is at work in the heart of every person, through the "seeds of the Word," to be found in human initiatives-including religious ones-and in humankind's efforts to attain truth, goodness and God himself. The Spirit offers the human race

71. See Congar, *I Believe in the Holy Spirit*.
72. John Paul II, *Dominum et Vivicantem*, sec. 53.

"the light and strength to respond to its highest calling"; through the Spirit, "humankind attains in faith to the contemplation and savoring of the mystery of God's design;" indeed, "we are obliged to hold that the Holy Spirit offers everyone the possibility of sharing in the Paschal Mystery in a manner known to God. Thus the Spirit, who "blows where he wills" (cf. Jn 3:8), who "was already at work in the world before Christ was glorified," and who "has filled the world . . . holds all things together [and] knows what is said" (Wis 1:7), leads us to broaden our vision in order to ponder his activity in every time and place . . . The Church's relationship with other religions is dictated by a twofold respect: "Respect for one in their quest for answers to the deepest questions of their life, and respect for the action of the Spirit in all . . . " "every authentic prayer is prompted by the Holy Spirit, who is mysteriously present in every human heart." This is the same Spirit who was at work in the Incarnation and in the life, death and resurrection of Jesus, and who is at work in the Church.[73]

73. John Paul II, *Redemptoris Missio*, secs. 28–29.

4

Non-Ordained—The Laity

The Second Vatican Council and the Laity

Certainly one of the signs of the times illuminated by the Holy Spirit at the Second Vatican Council was the recognition that the laity share in the redemptive work of Jesus and that their apostolates are a part of the salvific mission of the church.[1] The Spirit revealed that the laity are equally constitutive members of the church as the ordained and that their vocations and activities are more urgently, fervently, zealously, broadly, and intensely needed in the present circumstances due to the increase in population, progress in science and technology, and new problems confronting humanity.[2] The presence and actions of the church cannot be realized without the laity.[3] This is because the laity are united to Jesus and thereby given the right and duty to be apostles.[4] The Holy Spirit affords the laity special charisms for the purpose of building up the ecclesial body. It is the right and duty of the laity to exercise in freedom these gifts in the Church (*ad intra*) and in the world (*ad extra*) for the good of the church and all human beings.[5]

---

1. *Lumen Gentium,* sec. 33; *Apostolicam Actuositatem,* sec. 1
2. *Apostolicam Actuositatem,* secs. 1, 6; *Lumen Gentium,* secs. 30, 32, 36.
3. *Apostolicam Actuositatem,* sec. 1.
4. *Apostolicam Actuositatem,* sec. 3.
5. *Apostolicam Actuositatem,* sec. 3.

In light of Vatican II's teachings regarding the laity, the United States Conference of Catholic Bishops in their 1980 Pastoral Letter, *Called and Gifted*, taught that in order to bring to realization the Council's vision of the church as the people of God entrusted with being a sacrament of the kingdom of God, the laity are called to adulthood, holiness, ministry, community, and collaboration.[6] The laity are called to put to use their knowledge and charisms to imbue the church and the world with holiness, and to work in solidarity with the clergy to create effective ministries which, in turn, create effective Christian communities that afford an effective witness of the gospel unto the world.[7]

It can be said that the Second Vatican Council was "The Council of the Laity."[8] The ecclesiological vision inspired by the Spirit at Vatican II sinks or swims depending upon the laity living out their faith . . . or not. This is because the Council defined the very essence and nature of the church to be missionary,[9] sent out to be a sacrament,[10] pointing to and making present Jesus to the world. Such a vision can only succeed if the church's point of contact with the world—the laity—live out the faith in a manner that efficaciously points to and makes present Jesus, thereby impregnating the world with the values of the gospel and making an encounter with Jesus possible.[11]

Although the Second Vatican Council did much to advance the cause of the laity in the church, more still needs to be done. This is especially the case when it comes to advancing the laity's rightful role within the church's teaching, governing, and decision-making structures and mechanisms. The laity are endowed with gifts of the Spirit which enable them to share in the priestly, prophetic, and kingly ministries of Jesus. These spiritual gifts have implications for the laity's roles within the *ad intra* life of the church. As members of the *sensus fidelium* the laity are given gifts from the Spirit which make them sharers in the infallible charism of church. In light of these Spirit-given gifts and teachings of the church regarding the baptismal

6. Leckey, *Rediscovering Vatican II*, 56–59; see US Catholic Bishop's Pastoral Letter, *Called and Gifted*.

7. Leckey, *Rediscovering Vatican II*, 56–59.

8. Leckey, *Rediscovering Vatican II*, 1.

9. *Ad Gentes*, sec. 2.

10. *Sacrosanctum Concilium*, sec. 26; *Lumen Gentium*, secs. 1, 48; *Gaudium et Spes*, secs. 21, 42, 45; *Ad Gentes*, sec.5; Tkacik and McGonigle, *Pneumatic Correctives*, 1–4, 6–7.

11. *Apostolicam Actuositatem*, secs. 2, 3, 6, 7, 8; *Lumen Gentium*, secs. 31, 36.

dignity of the laity more needs to be done to afford the laity meaningful and substantive ways to share in the teaching, governance, and decision making of the church.

The church needs to develop institutional structures and mechanisms for the laity to exercise their Spirit-given roles in these ecclesial areas. Currently, no such structures and mechanisms exist. All that exists within the church are proposed collaborative vehicles for lay-cleric interaction. However, these vehicles lack meaningful and substantive authority for they are rendered to be consultative only and are at the discretion of the clergy. Such an ecclesial scenario is unacceptable to most of the students I teach given their level of education and democratic sensitivities.

During my time of diocesan service as secretary for ministries I was fortunate to work with a bishop who strived to advance the cause of the laity in meaningful and substantive ways, including at the level of ecclesial governance and decision making. The bishop's executive staff, which I was fortunate to be a member of, included three lay people, including a female chancellor. The bishop involved the entire staff in all processes of diocesan governance and decision making. This included having we laity participate in the diocesan consultors and personnel meetings. Such meetings are typically reserved for clergy only. Additionally, the bishop shared lunch with us every day. He used this time together to discuss governance of the diocese and to allow us all to become more intimate with one another. An incredible circle of trust was created. The bishop always discussed all matters pertinent to the diocese with us and solicited our thoughts on said matters. And the bishop listened, heard, and seriously considered each and all of our inputs. The bishop was not patronizing. He strove for consensus, drawing upon the wisdom of the staff as well as his own. Whenever he proffered his final determinations, he always afforded us the courtesy of discussing with us the reasons for his decisions. And, whenever his decisions were at odds with the input and counsel that any of us offered him, he always afforded us the courtesy of explaining his rationale and pastorally comforted and reassured us as well. This example of episcopal humility and leadership was exceptional to me. It was unlike anything else I was aware of occurring in a typical American diocese.

And yet, this experience was a unique one afforded three privileged lay members of the diocese by a bishop who governed in an exceptional manner. No such structures and mechanisms exist within the diocese for other laity to share in the governance of the diocese in such a meaningful and substantive way. The bishop did have a diocesan pastoral council composed largely of laity. However, this body is canonically deemed to be consultative only and serves only at the discretion of the bishop. Upon the bishop's retirement the council was dissolved and to my knowledge has not been reconstituted to date.

In light of the gifts of the Spirit unto ecclesial governance and decision making which the laity possess, the challenge becomes how do we create institutional structures and mechanisms which allow for the competencies and expertise of other lay members to inform the teachings and governance of the church? Now that I have returned full-time to my university position, as a lay person and theologian I too am no longer able to share in the ecclesial authority, governance, and decision making of the church. Devoid of ecclesial structures and mechanisms which involve the laity in meaningful and substantive ways laity are left to express themselves via ecclesial vehicles deemed only to be advisory and consultative. Such vehicles, furthermore, are left to the discretion of the clergy. Therefore, the laity are left with no institutional ways to express their authoritative Spirit-given voice to which Jesus appoints them via baptism.

Some may give voice to their views in writings such as this one but do so at the potential cost of being reprimanded and/or silenced. Others express themselves with their pocketbooks, withholding financial giving to the church. And others express themselves with their feet by leaving the church. This need not be the case. The church can do better. The church can honor what it teaches about the laity and what the Spirit and Jesus bestow upon the laity. The church can and must discern institutional structures and mechanisms which will allow the laity their rightful place and role within ecclesial authority, governance, and decision-making.

The Ecclesiological Vision of The Second Vatican Council and the Laity

For the laity to be effective witnesses of Jesus *ad extra* to the world they need to be animated, nourished, and sustained by the *ad intra* graces which the sacraments provide. Hence, the ecclesiological directives of the Second Vatican Council called for the *ad intra* reform of the church's sacramental life as a prerequisite for the church's *ad extra* apostolate of perpetuating the salvific and redemptive mission of Jesus out in the world. If the laity are to be effective witnesses of Jesus in the world pointing to and making present Jesus, the values of the gospel, and the marks and signs of the kingdom of God (if the church is to be an efficacious sacrament of Jesus in the world), then the laity need to be shaped, informed, empowered, nourished, and sustained by the grace which the sacraments communicate.[12] Hence, Vatican II's ecclesiological vision—focused upon the laity—called for the revision, reform, simplification, and inculturation of the church's *ad intra* sacramental life.[13] Such reform was seen by the Council fathers as necessary to the Church's *ad extra* missionary and sacramental apostolate to the world whereby an encounter with Jesus is made possible and the values of the gospel and kingdom of God come to infuse the temporal realm.

The first document promulgated at Vatican II was *the Decree on Liturgy (Sacrosanctum Concilium)*. This is because the *ad intra* liturgical life is the laity's primary point of contact with the church. Via the liturgical life of the church the laity receive the grace that the sacraments provide and that are needed if the laity are to live lives which point to and make present Jesus to the world (if the church is to be successful in its mission of being an efficacious sacrament of Jesus).[14] Hence, the ecclesiological vision of the Council begins with the *ad intra* reform of the church's sacramental life and a call for sacramental reforms that, above all else, ensure the full, conscious, and active participation of the laity in the *ad intra* sacramental economy of the church.[15]

Again, the church being an effective sacrament of Christ *ad extra* to the world depends upon the church's point of contact with the world—the laity—living lives which point to and make Jesus present. It follows, therefore, that the laity's point of contact with the church whereby they receive the grace needed to live a life of Christian witness within the world—the sacraments—be reformed. Such reforms will ensure the laity receive what

12. *Sacrosanctum Concilium*, secs. 2, 10, 41; *Lumen Gentium*, secs. 5, 33; *Apostolicam Actuositatem*, sec. 4; Tkacik and McGonigle, *Pneumatic Correctives*, 31–34, 46–49.

13. *Sacrosanctum Concilium*, secs. 37–40, 54; Tkacik and McGonigle, *Pneumatic Correctives*, 37.

14. *Lumen Gentium*, secs. 9–11, 13, 17, 33; *Apsotolicam Actuositatem*, secs. 3, 11; *Gaudium et Spes*, secs. 47–48, 52; John Paul II, *Christifideles Laici*, sec. 7; Tkacik and McGonigle, *Pneumatic Correctives*, 53–65.

15. *Sacrosanctum Concilium*, secs. 14, 30, 48; Tkacik and McGonigle, *Pneumatic Correctives*, 37.

they need—grace—to live efficacious lives of Christian witness and to be agents of gospel values and the kingdom of God in the world.[16]

The sacraments communicate the grace necessary for the laity to live lives of Christian witness and exercise apostolates of social justice *ad extra* in the world.[17] The sacraments afford the laity an encounter with Jesus who, in turn, they witness to others. Via the sacraments of baptism and confirmation the laity are appointed to the apostolates by the Lord himself.[18] Values of the kingdom of God and the gospel are also communicated within the *ad intra* sacramental life of the church.

Marriage and family life are the domestic church where the values of the gospel and kingdom of God and the principles of Catholic social thought are learned and practiced. As such marriage and family life serve as a primary and vital cell of the wider church and society.[19] The Eucharist recalls the Christ Event in songs, worship, narratives, prayers, and sacrament. The *ad intra* sacramental life of the church communicates grace as well as serves as a kind of school of social justice whereby the narratives, symbols, and rituals employed communicate the values of the gospel and kingdom of God.[20]

Receiving grace and assimilating the values communicated by the *ad intra* sacramental life of the church informs the vision, choices, actions, and character of the laity. It shapes the identity of the laity whereby they become Christian disciples empowered and sustained by grace to put into action the values they have made their own.[21] The *ad extra* ecclesiological vision of Vatican II called for the laity to live lives of Christian discipleship *ad extra* in the world. The *ad intra* sacramental life of the church makes Christian discipleship possible by shaping the character of the laity and

16. *Sacrosanctum Concilium,* secs. 2, 10; *Lumen Gentium* secs. 5, 33; *Apostolicam Actuositatem,* secs. 2, 3, 8; *Ad Gentes,* secs. 9, 15; Tkacik and McGonigle, *Pneumatic Correctives,* 31–34, 39–41, 46–49.

17. *Lumen Gentium,* secs. 5, 33; *Sacrosanctum Concilium,* secs. 2, 3, 6; *Apostolicam Actuositatem,* secs. 8, 10; *Ad Gentes,* secs. 9, 15, 36; Tkacik and McGonigle, *Pneumatic Correctives,* 39–41.

18. *Lumen Gentium,* secs. 7–8, 11–12, 31, 33; *Apostolicam Actuositatem,* sec. 3, John Paul II, *Christifideles Laici,* sec. 14; Tkacik and McGonigle, *Pneumatic Correctives,* 15–16, 19–28, 62–65.

19. *Gaudium et Spes,* secs. 47–48, 52; *Apostolicam Actuositatem,* secs. 11–12, *Gravitisimus Educationis,* sec. 3, John Paul II, *Familiaris Consortio,* secs. 21, 37, 42–43; and Tkacik and McGonigle, *Pneumatic* Correctives, 62–65.

20. Tkacik and McGonigle, *Pneumatic* Correctives, 34–37.

21. Tkacik, *Deacons and Vatican* II, 52–55.

affording them the grace needed to animate, nourish, and sustain their *ad extra* apostolates of justice in the world.[22]

The church's *ad extra* mission of being a sacrament of Jesus to the world can only be successful if the *ad intra* sacramental life of the church is first reformed. The laity—the church's point of contact with the world—should first receive what they need: grace—to be efficacious signs and symbols pointing to and making present Jesus and the values of the gospel and kingdom of God *ad extra* to the world. Hence, the Second Vatican Council took herculean steps to reform the church's *ad intra* sacramental life in ways and means that ensured that the laity were fully, consciously, and actively participating in the *ad intra* sacramental life.

As illustrative of the reforms undertaken by Vatican II to reform the church's *ad intra* sacramental economy to ensure the laity's full, conscious, and active participation were the Council's calls for revision and simplification of rites (particularly aimed at recovering the communal nature of sacramental celebrations and ensuring lay participation), liturgical inculturation, the use of the vernacular, and a softening of lay-cleric distinctions.[23] The laity were recognized as co-offering the Eucharist with the clergy and as lending to Eucharistic real presence via their corporate gathering, praise, *anamnesis*, and worship.[24] In short, the Council affirmed that the laity were necessary if the sacraments were to produce their full effects.[25]Even more pronounced than the steps taken to ensure the laity's participation in the church's *ad intra* sacramental life was the Council's consistent accentuation of the laity's indispensable *ad extra* apostolates of justice in the world.[26] Indeed, time and again the Council insists that it is the unique and particular duty and responsibility of the laity to live out their Christian witness via their vocations *ad extra* in the world.[27] At times the Council's accent upon the laity's *ad extra* apostolates and the secular nature of lay vocations tends to obscure the laity's *ad intra* ecclesial rights,

22. Tkacik, *Deacons and Vatican II*, 52–55.

23. *Sacrosanctum Concilium*, secs. 36–40, 54; Tkacik and McGonigle, *Pneumatic Correctives*, 37.

24. *Lumen Gentium*, secs. 10–11, *Sacrosanctum Concilium*, secs. 7 and 11; Tkacik and McGonigle, *Pneumatic Correctives*, 37–38.

25. *Sacrosanctum Concilium*, sec. 11; Tkacik and McGonigle, *Pneumatic Correctives*, 38.

26. *Lumen Gentium*, secs. 31, 33; *Apostolicam Actuositatem*, sec. 3; Tkacik and McGonigle, *Pneumatic Correctives*, 20–29, 53–61.

27. *Apostolicam Actuositatem*, secs. 2–4,7; *Lumen Gentium*, secs. 31 and 33.

duties, places, and roles. The ecclesiological vision of the Second Vatican Council simply cannot be actualized if the laity do not live out the faith *ad extra* within the world. The laity are the church's point of contact with the world whose vocations are lived in midst of the world. Consequently, the Council deemed that "one of the gravest errors of our time is the dichotomy between faith which many profess and the practice of their daily lives" and insisted that the professional and social activity of the laity not be opposed to their religious lives.[28]

> . . . the Church is not truly established and does not fully live, nor is a perfect sign of Christ unless there is a genuine laity . . . For the Gospel cannot become deeply rooted in the mentality, life and work of people without the active presence of lay people.[29]

Vatican II: The Laity and the Church-World Dialectic—A Pictorial

The ecclesiological vision of the Vatican II described above can be depicted as:

Backpack of our values and teachings of our faith that we take into the world. Catholic Social Teaching through our lived example.

Gospel: The Good News and visible example of Christ

Experiences of a diverse and pluralistic world

28. *Gaudium et Spes,* sec. 43.
29. *Ad Gentes Divinitus,* sec. 21.

On the left is the *ad intra* church. On the right is the *ad extra* world. In the middle, with one foot in the church and one foot in the world, is a lay person. Atop the head of the lay person is a halo demarcating their status as a graced and baptized member of the church endowed with unique and particular charisms from the Spirit called to live a life of holiness. This status is derived from participating in the Church's *ad intra* sacramental life. On the back of the lay person is a backpack full of the values of the gospel and kingdom of God and the principles of Catholic social thought.

These values and principles are learned within the *ad intra* ecclesial life. The dialectical arrows underneath represent the exchange which takes place between the church and world. This is the process of inculturation whereby the church offers the world the values of the gospel and the kingdom of God. The world, in return, offers the church diverse and pluralistic cultural experiences of human beings (philosophy, art, music, literature, science, technology, etc.) which lend to the church's ever-renewed efforts of evangelization in terms that are meaningful, relevant, and viable.[30] What the laity first receive from their *ad intra* ecclesial lives are grace, the values of the gospel and kingdom of God, and principles of Catholic social teaching. They are meant to witness these *ad extra* in the world via the various apostolates to which the Lord assigns them.

The church claims to the world that it is a sacrament. When the world gazes at the church it ought to be able to see and experience Jesus. Looking to the church the world looks through the laity who live within the world and whose vocations and apostolates are exercised within the world. Therefore, if the ecclesial claim of being a sacrament is to be efficacious, then the laity must be living their lives in the world in a manner that points to and makes present Jesus. Otherwise, the claim of the church is rendered a lie and the church's mission fails.

To live like Jesus and witness the values of the gospel and the kingdom of God within the world requires God's assistance. It requires grace. It also requires that the aforesaid values are manifested in a manner that speaks to all people, not just people of faith. The principles of Catholic social thought capture and convey the values of the gospel and the kingdom of God in a way that resonates with all people, not just people of faith. Therefore, the laity must begin *ad intra* the church proper so as to receive the grace of the

---

30. For consideration of the Church as a pilgrim sojourning amidst the diverse lived experiences of all people with the corresponding need for inculturation, see *Lumen Gentium*, secs. 9, 13, 17, 48; *Gaudium et Spes*, secs. 39–40, 44, 53, 57–58, 62; *Ad Gentes Divinitus*, secs. 16, 22; Tkacik and McGonigle, *Pneumatic Correctives*, 4–6.

sacraments and learn the values of the gospel and kingdom of God. However, these gifts received *ad intra* are meant to be shared with the world. The laity must fill their backpacks with the principles of Catholic social teaching and go forth *ad extra* to the world to unpack them via their various apostolates. The laity must also regularly return to the church *ad intra* so as to be perpetually renewed with the grace of the sacraments. This, in turn, empowers, animates, nourishes, and sustains their *ad extra* apostolates. The laity must also bring back to the church the lived and cultural experiences of the people of the world, as well as the developments in philosophy, art, music, literature, science, technology, etc. The church must perennially discover ways to give renewed expression to the values of the gospel and the kingdom of God in means that address the lived experience of people, and which are articulated in a manner that is meaningful, relevant, and viable to all. This dialectical exchange between the church and the world is the mandate that the church was commissioned by Jesus to do. It is the church's mission. It is how the church perpetuates the salvific and redemptive mission of Jesus. And the laity are at the center of the church's efforts. The laity ensure whether the church succeeds.

The Three-Fold Baptismal Dignities/Ministries of the Laity: Priest, Prophet, and King

Such an accent upon the laity and their role in ensuring the success of the church in its mission of extending the salvific and redemptive mission of Jesus and in ensuring the efficacy of the church's claim to be a sacrament of Jesus is unprecedented in the history of ecclesiology. As theologian Edward Sellner states, "At Vatican II the Roman Catholic Church for the first time in history took up the question of the status and roles of the laity and provided a theological perspective on Christian spirituality that takes seriously lay experiences, vocations and ministries."[31]

So, upon what is this accent on the laity based? The ecclesiological vision of the Second Vatican Council which places such an accent upon the indispensable and constitutive role of the laity is underpinned by the Council's affirmation of the three-fold baptismal dignity of the laity. Via baptism the laity are made sharers in the priestly, prophetic, and kingly

31. Sellner, "Lay Spirituality," 252.

ministries of Jesus by the Lord himself.[32] "What is clear is that the rubric of the three offices of Christ applied to the church was an attempt by Vatican II to break away from exclusively juridical notions of church," according to Fr. Ormond Rush.[33]

Each of these three dignities/ministries have corresponding *ad intra* and *ad extra* implications for the laity. The laity's *ad intra* priestly baptismal dignity implies greater participation of the laity in the church's *ad intra* sacramental life.[34] Recall the *ad intra* sacramental reforms undertaken by the Second Vatican Council discussed above. The laity's *ad extra* priestly baptismal dignity corresponds to the call to holiness that the laity are to exhibit *ad extra* in the world via their witness and apostolates.[35] As sharers in the prophetic dignity/ministry of Jesus via baptism, *ad intra* the laity are constituted members of the *sensus fidelium* whereby they share in the infallible teaching office of the church.[36] Sharing in the prophetic dignity/ministry of Jesus via baptism *ad extra* corresponds to the laity living lives which present the values of the gospel and kingdom of God in the world.[37] As sharers in the kingly dignity/ministry of Jesus via baptism, *ad intra* the laity ought to share in ecclesial governance and decision making.[38] Sharing in the kingly dignity/ministry of Jesus via baptism *ad extra* corresponds to the laity's apostolates of justice in the world.[39]

Among the six aspects/dimensions associated with the laity's three-fold baptismal dignity outlined above, the contemporary church has done an admirable job in promoting and advancing four. They are:

---

32. *Lumen Gentium,* sec. 31; Tkacik and McGonigle, *Pneumatic Correctives,* 19–20; Burkhard, "*Sensus Fidei*: Meaning, Role, and Future," 82–84; Epko, "*Sensus Fidelium* and the Threefold Office of Christ," 91–112.

33. Rush, *Vision of Vatican II,* 191.

34. John Paul II, *Christifideles Laici,* sec. 14; Tkacik and McGonigle, *Pneumatic Correctives,* 20–22; Congar, *Lay People in the Church,* 190–195, 213–216, 219, 222.

35. *Lumen Gentium,* secs. 41–42; Tkacik and McGonigle, *Pneumatic Correctives,* 21; Congar, *Lay People in the Church,* 190–195, 213–216, 219, 222.

36. *Lumen Gentium,* sec. 12, Tkacik and McGonigle, *Pneumatic Correctives,* 22–25; Congar, *Lay People in the Church,* 272–274, 288–289, 298; Rush, *Eyes of Faith,* 191.

37. Tkacik and McGonigle, *Pneumatic Correctives,* 22–25; Congar, *Lay People in the Church,* 190–5, 213–6, 219, 222.

38. Tkacik and McGonigle, *Pneumatic Correctives,* 25–27, 57–61; Congar, *Lay People in the Church,* 244–50; Rush, *Eyes of Faith,* 191.

39. *Lumen Gentium,* secs. 31, 33; *Apostolicam Actuositatem,* secs. 2–3, 5; Tkacik and McGonigle, *Pneumatic Correctives,* 26, 56–57; Congar, *Lay People in the Church,* 239.

1. The *ad intra* priestly baptismal dignity/ministries (greater participation of the laity in the church's *ad intra* sacramental economy)

2. The *ad extra* priestly baptismal dignity/ministries (call for the laity to live lives of holiness *ad extra* in the world)

3. The *ad extra* prophetic baptismal dignity/ministry whereby the laity are called to live lives which give witness to the values of the gospel and kingdom of God *ad extra* in the world

4. The *ad extra* kingly baptismal dignity/ministry associated with lay apostolates of justice in the world

However, the *ad intra* prophetic (which associates the laity with the *sensus fidelium* and infallible teaching authority of the church) and *ad intra* kingly (by which the laity ought to share in ecclesial governance and decision making) baptismal dignities/ministries have not been developed. The result is that the laity are deprived of their rightful place and role within the teaching authority of the church. Such is attested to by the absence of any formal institutional mechanisms, structures, and vehicles within the church by which the laity share in ecclesial authority, governance, and decision making. Such a scenario is unacceptable. Such a scenario not only fails to honor the laity's baptismal dignity, it also violates Catholic social teaching. It ignores the education, competencies/expertise, experiences, and charisms of the laity. It also fails to recognize the irrevocably diminished credibility of clerical ecclesial teaching, governance, and decision making in the wake of clergy abuse scandals and ecclesial cover-ups.

When is the time for the full dignity/ministries of the laity to be recognized, affirmed, and institutionally implemented within the church? When is the time for the laity to exercise their role within the teaching authority of the church as members of the *sensus fidelium*? When is the time for ecclesial institutional reform which afford laity mechanisms, vehicles, and structures to share in ecclesial governance and decision making? When is the time for the church to practice what it teaches regrading democratic and participatory forms of governance and subsidiarity? When is the time for the laity to be truly treated as equals, as adults whose education, competencies, expertise, and experiences are recognized, affirmed, utilized, and taken seriously? When? Now.

THE *SENSUS FIDELIUM* AND ECCLESIAL TEACHING AUTHORITY

Vatican II's *Dogmatic Constitution on the Church (Lumen Gentium)*, states:

> The holy people of God share also in Christ's prophetic office . . .
> The whole body of the faithful who have an anointing that comes
> from the holy one (1 John 2:20 and 27) cannot err in matters of
> belief. This characteristic is shown in the supernatural apprecia-
> tion of the faith (*sensus fidei*) of the whole people . . . By this ap-
> preciation of the faith, aroused and sustained by the Spirit of truth,
> the People of God . . . receives not the mere word of human beings,
> but truly the word of God (1 Thessalonians 2:13) . . . The people
> unfailingly adhere to this faith, penetrate it more deeply . . . and
> apply it more fully to daily life . . . By these gifts the Holy Spirit
> makes them fit and ready to undertake various tasks and offices for
> the renewal and building up of the Church . . . [40]

This incredible articulation of the laity's share in the prophetic dignity, ministry, and office of Jesus gives expression to the awesome *ad intra*
prophetic baptismal dignity bestowed upon the laity by the Lord himself.
This prophetic dignity empowers the laity to participate in ecclesial teaching, authority, governance, and decision-making in light of the charism of
infallibility they have as a result of the gift of the Holy Spirit (see above).

> By the gift of the Holy Spirit, "the Spirit of truth who comes from
> the Father," and bears witness to the Son (John 15:26), all of the
> baptized participate in the prophetic office of Jesus Christ . . . They
> are to bear witness to the Gospel and to the apostolic faith in the
> church and in the world. The Holy Spirit anoints them and equips
> them for that high calling, conferring on them a very personal
> and intimate knowledge of the faith of the church . . . As a result,
> the faithful have an instinct for the truth of the gospel . . . That
> supernatural instinct . . . is called the *sensus fidei*, and it enables
> Christians to fulfill their prophetic calling. [41]

Note how the laity's sense of the faith is supernatural (aroused and
sustained by the Holy Spirit), based upon the word of God (not human
beings), and is subject to the laity's ongoing discernment and application.
It is not something delegated or bestowed upon the laity by the clergy/
hierarchy. [42]

40. *Lumen Gentium*, sec. 12.

41. International Theological Commission, *Sensus Fidei Life of Church*, secs. 1–2.

42. Sullivan, *Magisterium*, 21.

The apostolic faith which constitutes the Christian tradition has been handed on throughout the generations of ecclesial history not only by Christian witness, preaching, and writings, but also through the way of life, prayer, and worship of every succeeding Christian generation. The faith, prayers, worship, communal life, and experience of the laity share in the church's perpetuation of the apostolic faith.[43] As Rush voices, the "*sensus fidelium* of the *sensus laicorum* (the sense of the laity) is a vital source for the Magisterium in discerning the lived faith of the church in different contexts throughout history: Christ fulfills this prophetic office, not only through the hierarchy . . . but also through the laity."[44]

> The importance of the *sensus fidei* in the life of the church was strongly emphasized by the Second Vatican Council. Banishing the caricature of an active hierarchy and a passive laity, and in particular the notion of a strict separation between the teaching church (*Ecclesia docens*) and the learning church (*Ecclesia discens*), the council taught that all the baptized participate in their own proper way in the three offices of Christ as prophet, priest and king. In particular, it taught that Christ fulfills his prophetic office not only by means of the hierarchy but also via the laity.[45]

Indeed, the very positioning of the chapter on the People of God prior to the chapter on the hierarchy in *Lumen Gentium* "marks a shift in Catholic teaching from depicting the laity in a derivative and passive relationship with the hierarchy in the mission of the church,"[46] notes Rush.

In his fine work, *The Eyes of Faith: The Sense of the Faithful and the Church's Reception of Revelation*, Ormand Rush posits that the *sensus fidelium* illuminates the church's faith as lived in midst of the world and assures "the church's reception of revelation throughout history—it enables the church to proclaim the Gospel in new times and cultures throughout history."[47]

Akin to the pneumatology of the Second Vatican Council, Rush suggests that the Holy Spirit, via the *sensus fidelium*, co-institutes the church

---

43. *Dei Verbum*, sec. 8; Sullivan, *Magisterium*, 11; International Theological Commission, *Sensus Fidei Life of Church*, sec. 41.

44. Rush, *Vision of Vatican II*, 306.

45. International Theological Commission, *Sensus Fidei Life of Church*, sec. 4; Rush, *Vision of Vatican II*, 3–4.

46. Rush, *Vision of Vatican II*, 187.

47. Rush, *Eyes of Faith*, 2.

via arousing and sustaining faith among Christian believers. The Holy Spirit also serves as the principle of reception in the process of revelation via the supernatural sense of the faith that the Spirit teaches all believers.[48] Vatican II's *Dogmatic Constitution on Divine Revelation (Dei Verbum)* describes revelation as the process whereby the loving triune God communicates to humanity, thereby drawing human beings into relationship.[49] The process of revelation and the Spirit's illumination of God's self-disclosure mediated by Jesus is first known and experienced by the *sensus fidelium*, i.e., the gift of faith provided by the Spirit to all believers. Reception of God's invitation to be drawn into the triune life requires human reception of revelation. Assistance from the Holy Spirit feeds this reception and the interpretive process as human beings assimilate revelation into their lives.[50] Rush posits that the canonical New Testament was generated and developed by the *sensus fidelium*.[51]

Hence, when speaking of the prophetic teaching office of the church, one ought to begin with the *sensus fidelium*, i.e., what the Spirit has made known to believers. As Rush says,

> It is the task of the prophetic office, which is the teaching office . . . to promote living witness to the Gospel by ensuring the vibrant link between doctrinal beliefs and the demands of a life of holiness in the contemporary world . . . Moreover, safeguarding the deposit of faith is the task of the whole People of God, a preservation guaranteed through the assistance of the Holy Spirit . . . faithful traditioning of the faith is not the Magisterium's exclusive preserve. It is the preserve of the whole church. *Dei Verbum section 8* speaks of the progress of the apostolic tradition by means of the Spirit's assistance to the *sensus fidelium* . . . [52]

It is the mission of the church and task of ecclesial teaching to articulate and perpetuate this, i.e., to hand on what the Spirit has made known to believers.[53] According to Rush, "Reception and tradition are two correlative aspects of the one continuous mission of the church: what is received must be handed on, and what is handed on must then be received anew if

48. Rush, *Eyes of* Faith, 26, 29, 38; *Dei Verbum*, sec. 2.

49. *Dei Verbum*, sec. 6.

50. Rush, *Vision of Vatican II*, 26–28.

51. Rush, *Vision of Vatican II*, 85, 91–172.

52. Rush, *Vision of Vatican II*, 59–60.

53. Rush, *Vision of Vatican II*, 40.

it is to be effectively traditioned to new generations in new cultures and contexts."[54]

It is the Spirit, via the *sensus fidelium*, which enables reception of revelation in new contexts throughout human history by making known the meaning and truth of God's revelation through Jesus for a particular time and place.[55] Therefore, inculturation and an openness to a diversity of ideas about revelation are necessary if the church is to effectively perpetuate the truths of revelation in new cultures and contexts.[56]

> Inculturated forms of the faith, especially in local churches, constitute a horizon of understanding within which the faith tradition from the past is encountered and received. This reception however, is a mutually critical one, in which the faith of the local church is shaped in part by the tradition from the past, and whereby the tradition from the past is reinvigorated and changed (or challenged) by the peculiarities of the local church culture. The *sensus fidelium* comes into play here in that no such encounter can be rendered in abstraction from the ongoing experience of the faith in particular social, political, and cultural contexts of the local church . . . the magisterium could not and never has obviated the *a priori* role of the *sensus fidelium* which has resulted from living the faith in particular historical circumstances.[57]

In short, according to Paul Crowley, SJ., "the principle of reception enables effective traditioning."[58] Such is the example and model of the New Testament and apostolic faith communities.[59] As revelation is received in different cultures and contexts the church's catholicity is ensured. Again Rush, echoing Vatican II, speaks of the local churches as being the *loci receptionis*, i.e., places of reception, where the Spirit enables the appropriation of revelation in their particular *locus* and where the "Spirit enables those churches to understand and interpret their experience of salvation from the perspective of their particular locus."[60] Thus, it is the Spirit, via the *sensus*

---

54. Rush, *Vision of Vatican II*, 40.

55. Rush, *Vision of Vatican II*, 41.

56. Rush, *Vision of Vatican II*, 41; Soede, "*Sensus Fidelium* and Moral Discernment," 229–233.

57. Crowley, "Catholicity, Inculturation, and Newman's *Sensus Fidelium*," 66.

58. Crowley, "Catholicity, Inculturation, and Newman's *Sensus Fidelium*," 53.

59. Crowley, "Catholicity, Inculturation, and Newman's *Sensus Fidelium*," 53, 64–65.

60. Rush, *Vision of Vatican II*, 50.

fidelium, "who stimulates the manifold ways in which the saving Gospel is inculturated and contextualized throughout the world."[61]

Hierarchical magisterial teachings ought to be informed by and give expression to what the Spirit has made known to and received by the *sensus fidelium*. JMR Tillard, OP, states,

> Cut off from this essential reference to a "lived truth" which in a way precedes and conditions it, the act of the Roman Magisterium involved in what is called "dogmatic definition" has no meaning anymore . . . For the *sensus fidelium* constitutes as it were the material which is taken up and refined in the "definition" . . . the Magisterium should draw from the very life of the people of God the reality to be discerned, judged, and promulgated or "defined." For it has to exercise all its activity upon the word as received and lived in the Church.[62]

Revelation and faith are matters of a dialectical relationship between the triune God and human beings, not doctrinal propositions formulated and articulated by hierarchical magisterial authorities separate from the pluralistic lived experiences of the people. In exercising its prophetic teaching office the church needs to go beyond a purely propositional statement of intellectual meaning to include transformative praxis which directly responds to the question to constitute an effective answer.[63] As Rush points out, "according to *Lumen Gentium* 12, the church's infallibility in believing is rooted in the *sensus fidei* of the whole People of God."[64]

Being constituted as part of the *sensus fidelium* by the Holy Spirit through one's baptismal prophetic dignity, believers are endowed with an imaginative capacity. Rush calls this an *organon* of faith, whereby the faithful receive and make sense of God reaching out to them and make sense of the significance of this for their lives.[65] He states, "We might speak of the *sensus fidei* as a faculty or organon for interpreting the past, giving shape to Christian identity in the present, and envisaging future possibilities."[66]

The laity, as members of the *sensus fidelium*, are endowed by the Spirit with a gift which enables them to receive, interpret, understand, and apply

---

61. Rush, *Vision of Vatican II*, 50.
62. Tillard, "*Sensus Fidelium*," 32, 49.
63. Rush, *Vision of Vatican II*, 75.
64. *Lumen Gentium*, sec. 12; Rush, *Vision of Vatican II*, 39.
65. Rush, *Vision of Vatican II*, 66–67.
66. Rush, *Vision of Vatican II*, 68–69, 241–3, 255, 294.

revelation vis –a-vis their respective cultures, contexts, and diverse experiences. Therefore, the laity have a pneumatically constituted place and role within the prophetic teaching function of the church—the most fundamental place where revelation is first received, interpreted, assimilated, and applied to life.[67] The laity, therefore, ought to have places and roles within the institutional structures, mechanisms, and vehicles of the church whereby their teaching substantively informs magisterial teachings. "The lay faithful's sense of the faith . . . must be allowed to contribute to, in some way, the formal judgment and the official formulation of church teaching," according to Rush.[68]

This is because whatever the bishops and pope proclaim is the faith of the whole church.[69] Given that individuals always experience from a particular horizon, one's view and perspective is always limited due to the cultural, social, historical, scientific, economic, technological, and philosophical conditions of their respective situation.[70] This is true of we believers now, and it was true for all past believers. Therefore, ecclesial teachings, such as those regarding women and homosexuality, ought to be viewed as conditioned and limited by the cultural and historical situations in which the church stands. "Contemporary praxis of a particular past belief may indeed change from generation to generation, from one context to another," states Rush.[71]

Ongoing adaptation and renewal (*aggiornamento*) must be a guiding ecclesial principle. Certain structures and teachings which corresponded to the needs and which illumined questions of prior ages may no longer do so in contemporary situations. Such teachings and structures must be recast to address modern needs and questions. Pneumatic correctives may be warranted. The truths of the Christian faith are neither absolute nor relative in their expression, rather they are pneumatic, i.e., they are formed and guided by the Holy Spirit in their meaning, interpretation, and application. They may need to change, and they may need to take diverse and pluralistic expressions within the church which is catholic, i.e., one yet apostolic.[72]

---

67. Rush, *Vision of Vatican II*, 69.

68. Rush, *Vision of Vatican II*, 195, 222.

69. Rush, *Vision of Vatican II*, 201.

70. Rush, *Vision of Vatican II*, 71, 74.

71. Rush, *Vision of Vatican II*, 77.

72. Tkacik and McGonigle, *Pneumatic Correctives*, 2–3.

It is the experience of the laity, as members of the *sensus fidelium*, who have been gifted by the Spirit to receive, interpret, understand, and apply God's revealed invitation to a loving a relationship. As Rush states, "It is this application of the Gospel to daily life, in new contexts and cultures, that constitutes the fundamental role of the laity in the traditioning of revelation and the particular contribution to the teaching office of their sense of faith as lay people."[73]

It is lay people who attempt to discern what is of God in contemporary life; who face issues which require interpretation, evaluation, and response; and who intuitively sense how the faith ought to be applied to the signs of the times.[74] What may have been understood as impediments to a relationship with God in the past—due to the limitations inherent to the respective horizons of the faithful at the time—may no longer be deemed impediments now. Such is the case, I propose, vis-à-vis women's ordination, homosexuality, and laity sharing in ecclesial authority, governance, and decision making within the contemporary American church. Given the level of education among the laity, American sensitivities regarding women, and the participatory and democratic nature of our political system, these are no longer impediments. In the words of Giuseppe Angelini, "In response to unsatisfactory aspects of the responses given by the magisterium to the new moral problems, especially those concerning the sphere of sexual behavior, modern theology makes a precise accusation: the magisterium ignores the *sensus fidelium*."[75]

It ought to be clear that I appeal to the laity as members of the *sensus fidelium* and their reception, interpretation, understanding, and effort to apply and live out God's revelation of love as underlying the ordination of women and acceptance of homosexuality within the experience of the American church. Consistent with what Rush posits,

> In the ongoing divine-human dialogue facilitated by the Spirit's organon, new questions arise in human history for which former divine-human dialogue has not given answers . . . It is the Spirit, the principle of reception who enables the church to find new answers and new solutions to new questions and new challenges . . .
> 76

---

73. Rush, *Vision of Vatican II*, 253; *Lumen Gentium*, 35.

74. Rush, *Vision of Vatican II*, 259.

75. Angelini, "*Sensus Fidelium* and Moral Discernment," 235.

76. Rush, *Vision of Vatican II*, 296.

As the *sensus fidelium* receives and traditions the faith throughout history in different cultures and contexts, "oftentimes reasons cannot be given for this sense of faith . . . but love knows what love must do,"[77] notes Rush.

Although the notion of the *sensus fidelium* is underpinned by and finds its roots in scripture and has been taught by the church throughout the patristic, medieval, scholastic, and reformation periods of ecclesial history,[78] it has failed to be integrated into the *de facto* existential praxis of ecclesial authority, governance, and decision making in any meaningful and substantive way. Alas, as one observes the functioning of the Roman Catholic Church one would never know that the laity have such a prophetic dignity. One would not know that the laity have the right and duty to share ecclesial authority, governance, and decision making. One would not know that the laity possess the charism of infallibility in matters pertaining to the faith.

How can this be? And why are the laity complicit vis-à-vis ecclesial institutional exercise of authority, governance, teaching, and decision making which totally and categorically jettisons them and deprives them their rightful and charismatically gifted place, role, and function within these aspects of ecclesial life? Why is this theology of prophetic baptismal dignity and the *sensus fidelium* not more widely taught and understood? Why are the church's *de facto* institutional structures, mechanisms, and vehicles totally devoid of ways and means for the laity to exercise their rightful place and role within ecclesial authority, governance, teaching, and decision-making? Why is the church's praxis not consistent with and faithful to its theology and teachings regarding the baptismal prophetic dignity of the laity and the *sensus fidelium*? Why do the laity tolerate such a situation, particularly educated laity within the democratic context of contemporary America?

When is the time for the church to practice what it teaches about the laity and their rightful place and role within the institutional church's authority, governance, teaching, and decision making? When is the time for the laity to be outraged by their subordination and exclusion from ecclesial authority, governance, teaching, and decision-making? When is the time for the laity to claim what is gifted to them by Jesus via baptism and charisms of the Spirit? When? Now.

77. Rush, *Vision of Vatican II*, 238–9.

78. International Theological Commission, *Sensus Fidei in Life of Church*, sec. 8; Rush, *Vision of Vatican II*, 16–26, 64–65.

Catholic Social Teaching and Ecclesial Decision Making—Democratic, Participatory, and Respectful of Subsidiarity

The prophetic baptismal and kingly dignity bestowed on the laity by the Lord constitutes them as ecclesial members endowed with the Holy Spirit's charism of infallibility and a supernatural appreciation vis-à-vis matters of belief and faith.[79] The pneumatic corrective required of the church today in terms of honoring this dignity and charism of the laity *ad intra* is further supported by magisterial teachings of recent decades. Models of governance marked by shared responsibility, decision making, and authority have been consistently heralded by the magisterium in recent decades. The magisterium has defined participation and equality as basic forms of human dignity and freedom. It has consistently identified participation in governance as a fundamental human right. It has acknowledged democratic forms of decision making most consistent with human nature. And it has cited that the practice of subsidiarity ought to be a guiding principle in all collegial efforts.[80] The very integrity of these church teachings demands that such principles which the church expects and demands of other institutions be embraced by and applied to the church also. Double standards, hypocrisy, and duplicity are unacceptable and undermine the church's credibility. Given that these principles have been linked to human nature and dignity, the church, which is to be the champion *par excellent* of human nature and dignity, must walk the talk and practice what it preaches lest its credibility be compromised.

Historically the church has tended to exonerate itself from such principles that it expects from other institutions by juxtaposing itself as a pneumatological entity as opposed to secular entities. However, once the magisterium associated the principles with human nature and dignity the church can no longer differentiate itself in a manner that would excuse it from honoring, championing, and actualizing that which the church must be the greatest proponent and advocate of. The church must be the institutional exemplar which honors human dignity and the rights which stem from the social and relational nature of human beings.

---

79. *Lumen Gentium*, sec. 12.

80. Pius XI, *Quadragesimo Anno*, sec. 79; John XXIII, *Mater et Magistra*, sec. 53; Paul VI, *Octogesima Adveniens*, secs. 4, 22, 24, 47, 50; *Gaudium et Spes*, secs. 31, 65, 68, 73, 75; John Paul II, *Centesimus Annus*, secs. 46, 48; Tkacik and McGonigle, *Pneumatic Correctives*, 65–67; Tkacik, *Deacons and Vatican II*, 71, 121–122.

Unless the church demonstrates the courage to adapt these principles to its own structures and institutional mechanisms of power, then its advocacy of human dignity and call for subsidiarity will be rendered void of credibility. Above all, if the church is to be a sacrament of the Paschal Mystery of Jesus, then it must evidence the veracity of its teachings first and foremost in its own example.[81]

According to John Burkhard, OFM Conv, "An increased awareness of the implications of the *sensus fidei* for the role of the laity today can help the . . . church come to terms with issues of democratization within the church . . . Co-responsibility based on a profound sense of the *sensus fidei* might also include appropriate ecclesiastical forms whereby the laity can express their views on a whole range of issues."[82]

When is the time for the church to practice what it preaches in terms of human dignity and nature as it applies to the laity and their rightful baptismal dignity vis-à-vis participating in *ad intra* ecclesial governing, authority, and decision-making? When? Now.

As the laity come to know and own their baptismal dignity and role as the *sensus fidelium* afforded to them by the Lord, and as they come to learn what the church itself teaches about participatory and democratic forms of governance, shared decision making and governance, authority, and subsidiarity, the laity ought to expect and demand institutional ecclesial reform. The laity ought to be outraged that they, the overwhelming majority of ecclesial members, are categorically jettisoned from participating in ecclesial governance, authority, and decision- making. This will be even more so given that the laity are often as educated, or more educated, than some clergy, and in light of the fact that among the laity there are members of the church whose competency and expertise in certain matters of theological, moral, and/or pastoral importance exceeds that of the clergy.

The Education, Competency, Expertise, and Experience of the Laity—Collaboration must be Greater than Consultation

The time has also come for the church to practice—in meaningful, substantive, and serious ways—what it teaches when it comes to the education, competencies, expertise, and experiences of the laity, and what ought to

81. Tkacik and McGonigle, *Pneumatic Correctives*, 66.
82. Burkhard, "*Sensus Fidei*: Meaning, Role and Future," 87.

be corresponding ecclesial collaboration and shared authority, governance, and decision-making.[83] In light of the laity's *ad intra* kingly baptismal dignity, conversion in terms of the church's mentality, attitudes, and disposition regarding the laity's place and role within the authority and governance of the church must occur. Ecclesial institutional structures, mechanisms, and vehicles must be developed and implemented *ad intra* which ensure—with integrity and substance—the laity's place and role in the *de facto* authority, governance, and decision making of the church. For example, canonical visits to parishes, diocesan synods, and pastoral councils need to be revamped.[84] And, as was the case in the past, the consent of the laity in matters pertaining to ecclesial appointments is to be required and they are to be present and active at ecumenical councils. Canon Law mandates certain ecclesial bodies comprised of laity that need to be revamped as well. Such examples will need to be renewed, reformed, and expanded so as to honor and implement the laity's *ad intra* kingly dignity bestowed upon them by Jesus.

Such renewed, reformed, and expanded institutional structures ensuring meaningful participation of the laity in shared ecclesial authority and governance will have to go far beyond the mere consultative status they historically and currently have. Collaboration will need to go beyond the clergy simply listening to the laity and dialoguing with them.[85] Renewed, reformed, and expanded institutional structures, mechanisms, and vehicles which ensure that the laity participate in ecclesial decision making in substantive ways will have to afford the laity real teeth and authentic power. Ecclesial authority, governance, and decision making will need to be marked by a healthy dialectic whereby the laity and clergy mutually condition one another. The church will need to implement ways of arriving at a "collective consciousness" to arrive at consensus via consultation, dialogue, and synodal decision-making processes in the church.[86] In the words of Guiseppe Angelini, "The *sensus fidei* can make a decisive contribution to the elaboration of moral knowledge; but if it is to achieve this, it must take on an objective form in the context of the church."[87]

---

83. Wijlens, "*Sensus Fidelium*—Authority Protecting And Promoting," 113–38.

84. Wijlens, "*Sensus Fidelium*—Authority Protecting And Promoting," 128.

85. US Catholic Bishops Pastoral Letter, *Called and Gifted*, sec. 9

86. McCann, "Karl Rahner and the *Sensus Fidelium*," 164–7.

87. Angelini, "*Sensus Fidelium* and Moral Discernment," 238.

When is the time to move past an ecclesiology which demarcates an active teaching church—clergy—and a passive listening Church—laity? When is the time for the church to move beyond clerical-lay collaboration in terms of listening, dialogue, and consultation which can be tuned out, muted, and unilaterally rejected by the clergy? When? Now. If the church continues to call for lay advice and contributions to the work of the church only to exclude the laity from ecclesial authority, governance, and decision making, the laity are continued to be rendered second class members of the ecclesial community.[88]

When is the time to move beyond patronizing and condescending instructions regarding the collaboration of the non-ordained faithful in the sacred ministry of priests which are dismissive of laity due to their "secular character"; their diminished participation in the dignity of Jesus in both "essence" and "degree;" and the laity's alleged lack of sacred power and inability to act in the person of Jesus and perpetuate the faith of the apostles?[89] When? Now. For such characterizations only serve to perpetuate a subordination of the laity and disregard for the *sensus fidelium*. They reduce the laity to limited roles and functions according to prescriptions, provisions, permissions, conditions, and admittances proffered by clergy, justified by a clerical elitism which posits ordination in terms of power rather than service.[90]

The right and duty of the laity to participate in the *ad intra* life of the church in all of its aspects and dimensions is not a matter of delegation from clergy, nor exceptional circumstances determined, permitted, or prescribed by clergy.[91] Rather it comes from their ecclesial equality and divine appointment to the church's apostolates. The Vatican's *Instruction on Certain Questions Regarding the Collaboration of the Non-Ordained Faithful in the Sacred Ministry of Priest* perpetuates patronizing and condescending lines of thought in regard to the laity such as those articulated above. It perpetuates a mentality, attitude, and disposition towards the laity which are, quite frankly, offensive, and which continue to reduce the laity to consultative roles and perpetuate the lack of deliberate ecclesial

88. Kung, *Reforming the Church*, 75; Tkacik and McGonigle, *Pneumatic Correctives*, 60.

89. See Congregation Doctrine of Faith, *Instruction Certain Questions Regarding Collaboration Non-Ordained Faithful*.

90. See Congregation Doctrine of Faith, *Instruction Certain Questions Regarding Collaboration Non-Ordained Faithful*.

91. See *Instruction Certain Questions Regarding Collaboration Non-Ordained Faithful*.

structures, appointments, and participation[92] which would afford the laity their rightful place and roles within ecclesial authority, decision- making, and sacramental praxis.

All baptized members of the church share a common kingly dignity. As noted in *Lumen Gentium,* "There is in Christ and in the Church no inequality . . . all share a true equality with regard to the dignity and to the activity common to all the faithful for building up the body of Christ."[93]

Therefore, clergy and laity are bound to one another by a mutual and unifying purpose.[94] Consequently, the clergy must:

> . . . recognize and promote the dignity as well as well as the responsibilities of the laity in the church . . . Let them willingly make use of their prudent advice . . . allowing them freedom and room for action . . . Further, let them encourage the laity so that they may undertake this task on their own initiative . . . In this way, the whole church, strengthened by each one of its members, can more effectively fulfill its mission for the life of the world.[95]

Note how such shared ecclesial authority, governance, and decision making is linked to the mission of the church to the world and its efficacy of being a sacrament to the world. Clergy owe respect and deference towards the laity not only in light of the common baptismal kingly dignity all members of the church share, and the laity's central role in the mission of the church (see above), but also because the laity have wisdom, competencies, and expertise vis-à-vis signs of the times due to their experiences and education that the clergy do not have.[96] Therefore, again, clergy should recognize the laity's right and duty to play their part in building up the church.[97]

Such a shift in ecclesial exercise of authority, governance, and decision making is also consistent with wider ecclesiological emphases and impetuses illuminated by the Spirit at Vatican II, namely the Council's accentuation of local churches, collegiality, synodality, and subsidiarity. All of these suggest de-centralized exercise of ecclesial authority which defers to local competencies. Such a shift likewise is consistent with the council's

92. See *Instruction Questions Collaboration of Non-Ordained Faithful.*

93. *Lumen Gentium,* sec. 12.

94. *Lumen Gentium,* sec. 12.

95. *Lumen Gentium,* sec. 37.

96. *Presbyterorum Ordinis,* sec. 9.

97. *Christus Dominus,* sec. 16.

tendency to discuss the exercise of hierarchical authority in terms of service and pastoral shepherding to the people of God. Such service is called to promote and to facilitate the participation of all in the mission of the church, particularly through participation in the three dignities/ministries/offices of Jesus.[98] When is the time for institutional realization, actualization, and implementation of what the Spirit said to the church about the non-ordained at the Second Vatican Council? When? Now.

---

98. *Lumen Gentium*, sec. 27; *Christus Dominus*, sec.16; Rush, *Vision of Vatican II*, 289–91, 295–6, 300–301.

5

CONCLUSION

I THANK YOU FOR reading this book. I hope that it provided some kind of aid or comfort. The topics considered are ones that I believe mark the signs of the times of the contemporary Catholic Church in the United States. It is such signs of the times as these that the Holy Spirit called upon the church at the Second Vatican Council to consider and address vis-à-vis the gospel example of Jesus, in conversation with the lived experience of the faithful. The discernment of what the Spirit is saying to the church is ongoing. Efforts to understand and communicate what the Spirit is asking of us are also ongoing. The lived experience of the faithful as well as the evolution and developments of our understandings pertinent to gender, sexuality, religious pluralism, and the laity lend to such efforts. The Spirit illuminates what is meaningful, relevant, and viable to the ongoing life of the church. It is our task to respond to these promptings of the Spirit in fidelity. This is true even if our faithful response to the Spirit requires that we die to previous ways of believing, thinking, and acting. As Dietrich Bonhoeffer noted, faithful obedience to the demands of the gospel may prove to be costly. Let us be open to what the Spirit might be saying. Let us pray for the courage to respond in fidelity. Ecclesiological dualisms which polarize and divide will need to be abandoned out of a spirit of *kenosis* (self-emptying love) in conformity to the example of Jesus. If we are to receive what the Spirit is saying, we will have to discern together—women and men, gay and straight, Catholics and other believers, laity and clergy. We will have to collaborate and cooperate with one another. We will have to honor, respect, and heed the charisms, competencies, and expertise of all through whom the Spirit enlightens faith and praxis, and illuminates the way. *Maranatha* (come Holy Spirit).

WOMEN

In the United States, as well as in areas across the world, women are more and more assuming functions of leadership, both in the church and wider society. What is being sought is what Leonardo Boff referred to as an "equality in difference."[1] Several societies have evolved to the point where authority is expected to be enjoyed by either member of the human couple in which respect afforded to the other is exercised with personal equality, not differentiations based on what is deemed to be functions of one of the sexes. A change of consciousness has emerged in the relationship between the sexes which allows for the emergence of women as persons rather than circumscribing them by exclusive determinations proffered in light of functions.[2] The broadening personalization of women is surely consistent with the radical equality between women and men as the image and likeness of God together, not separately. This is what Jesus and subsequent Christian anthropology accentuate and affirm.

As I was working on this book the one-hundredth anniversary of the ratification of the nineteenth amendment to the United States Constitution, which gave women the right to vote, was celebrated on August 18, 2020. Furthermore, we gained the first female vice president of the United States. Just as American society, customs, and praxis have evolved to recognize, affirm, and honor the dignity and rightful roles of women so too it is past time for the Catholic Church to do the same. When? Now.

As Boff notes, it is Jesus' attitude that "provides a permanent critique of the church, or any other institution, were it to happens to persist in its discrimination against women merely by reason of the fact that they are women."[3] For Jesus defended the equality of women and men, maintained that women are human persons, and opposed those who sought to reduce women to the status of objects.[4] Jesus' ethical preaching called for the liberation of all human beings from legalistic and discriminatory subjugation, delivered human beings from the burdens of sinful pasts, illuminated new

1. Boff, *Ecclesiogenesis*, 76.
2. Boff, *Ecclesiogenesis*, 77.
3. Boff, *Ecclesiogenesis*, 79.
4. Boff, *Ecclesiogenesis*, 79.

possibilities of reconciliation and communion, and made possible new forms of solidarity among human beings.[5]

The Christian message is not exhausted by any historical articulation, rather it is limited. Therefore it can be transcended, enriched, and corrected.[6] Jesus stressed that which transcends all human divisions. As Boff states, "Indeed, he expressly excluded the biological, sexual factor as meaningful in the determination of human persons: 'Who is my mother? Who are my brothers? . . . Whoever does the will of my heavenly father is brother and sister and mother to me,'" (Matthew 12:48–50).[7]

Whoever accepted Jesus he empowered to become children of God (See John 1:12). According to Boff, "Therefore, to appeal to Christ's maleness in order to justify the privilege of the male sacerdotal ministry (ordained priesthood) is to argue from biology, and thereby to abandon any historical fidelity to Jesus."[8]

A person represents Christ and acts on Jesus' behalf on behalf of the church not by virtue of biological factors, but by virtue of faith.[9] When is the time for the church to truly embrace this fact and allow women to be ordained? Now.

In the decades since the Second Vatican Council the work of feminist theologians like Phyllis Trible, Elisabeth Schussler Fiorenza, and Elizabeth Johnson have brought to light the riches of the Spirit that the "woman-church"[10] has to offer Christian faith communities. They have shown us how to recover the "repressed memories"[11] of women to discover a "usable past"[12] within Christianity that can serve as a "prototype for women's

---

5. Boff, *Ecclesiogenesis*, 79–80, 82.

6. Boff, *Ecclesiogenesis*, 82, 84, 87.

7. See Boff, *Ecclesiogenesis*, 82.

8. See Boff, *Ecclesiogenesis*. Parenthesis mine.

9. Boff, *Ecclesiogenesis*, 83.

10. A movement of women and women-identified men whose commitment and mission is one of solidarity with women who suffer the triple oppressions of sexism, racism, and poverty.

11. The contributions of women to biblical salvation history and Christian tradition which have been lost or thwarted due to patriarchal domination and androcentric thinking.

12. Aspects from scripture and the tradition which lend to the salvation, liberation, and freedom of all.

liberation"[13] in the contemporary church.[14] They have illuminated biblical scholarship marked by precision of language and terms, and intellectual honesty. They have helped us to speak of, symbolize, and understand God in ways that do justice to the inexhaustible mystery of God which include feminine images, symbols, and concepts. In doing so they have steered the church away from patriarchy and androcentrism which have historically compromised the tradition's understanding of the divine mystery. They have cautioned against the tendency toward idolatry which absolutizes male images, symbols, and concepts which in turn limit our understanding of God and impede us from viewing women equally as the image and likeness of God.[15] When is the time for their contributions to be recognized, honored, and implemented into the lived experience of the contemporary church? When? Now.[16]

HOMOSEXUALITY

In Chapter Two I spoke of the work of Father James Martin, SJ, who is working to build bridges between the church and the LGBTQ+ community. Shortly before I began writing this book Father Martin met with Pope Francis. All indications are that the pope offered affirmation and support to Father Martin and his ministerial efforts.[17] On other occasions the pope has suggested that it is not for others to judge the status of gay persons before God, rather to accompany them.[18] He has suggested that God is the creator of all persons, gay and straight.[19] The pope has received and communed groups of LGBTQ+ visitors[20] and has said that there is no place for homophobia within the church.[21] Rather, the church should provide a space

13. Accepting as inspired only that which lends to the salvation, liberation, and freedom of all.

14. See Fiorenza, *In Memory of Her.*

15. See Johnson, *She Who Is.*

16. The Sisters of Saint Joseph of Carondolet provide an example of women within the church speaking truth unto power via their letter to Cardinal Dolan articulating their concerns regarding the Cardinal's praise of President Trump. See Sisters of Charity of New York, "Leadership Team Shares Concerns."

17. NCR Editorial Staff, "The Pope is Not Upset with Fr. James Martin."

18. McElwee, "Francis Explains Who Am I to Judge."

19. DeBernardo, "From Who Am I to Judge God Made You Like This."

20. See Shine, "Pope Meets with LGBT Pilgrims."

21. See Shine, "No Place for Homophobia."

for the LGTBQ+ community and dialogue with them.[22] Additionally, even as I was writing this book, many episcopal bishops and priests in Germany were suggesting that gay couples who live in faithfulness ought to have their relationships blessed by the church.[23] Cardinal Jean-Claude Hollerich of Luxembourg went so far as to suggest that it was time for a fundamental revision of church teaching on homosexuality in light of new sociological and scientific understandings.[24]

Although much inconsistency can be found in the pope's and the various national episcopal conferences around the world on the issue of homosexuality, it also seems as if the lived experience of the faithful and the Holy Spirit are challenging the church to look upon the issue with a new sense of human relationships and a new pastoral attitude and disposition. When is the time for all Christians to do the same? Now. Let us pray that, no matter what is to be made of the morality of homogenital physical sex acts, there is conversion of hearts and minds when it comes to truly recognizing and respecting everyone as the image, likeness, and child of God. Let our language and pastoral disposition toward all people be merciful and loving. Let there be no more disparaging and denigrating rhetoric and characterizations of gays. No longer should one who is gay feel forced to live in shame, secrecy, and fear. No longer should their employment and status within the church be at risk if found out. When? Now.

Indeed, as Daniel Horan surmised, if the church fails to reform its discriminatory practices against and mistreatment of LGBTQ+ persons history will come to judge the church's attitudes and behaviors as indefensible and reprehensible.[25]

ECUMENISM AND INTERRELIGIOUS DIALOGUE

Pope John Paul II conveys well my sentiments regarding the incredible advances made in the areas of ecumenical and interreligious dialogue in the decades since Vatican II:

> What shall I say of all the initiatives that have sprung from the new ecumenical orientation? The unforgettable Pope John XXIII

22. DeBarnardo, "Pope Advice to Parents Gay People."

23. Rocca, "German Catholic Leaders Support Blessings."

24. See Nachrichten-Agentur, "EU Cardinal Call for Change."

25. See Horan, "History Will Judge the Church."

set out the problem of Christian unity with evangelical clarity as a simple consequence of the will of Jesus Christ himself, our Master, the will that Jesus stated on several occasions but to which he gave expression in a special way in his prayer in the Upper Room the night before he died: "I pray . . . Father . . . that they may all be one." The Second Vatican Council responded concisely to this requirement with its Decree on Ecumenism . . . To all who, for whatever motive, would wish to dissuade the Church from seeking the universal unity of Christians the question must once again be put: Have we the right not to do it? Can we fail to have trust-in spite of all human weakness and all the faults of past centuries-in our Lord's grace as revealed recently through what the Holy Spirit said and we heard during the Council? If we were to do so, we would deny the truth concerning ourselves . . . What we have just said must also be applied-although in another way and with the due differences-to activity for coming closer together with the representatives of the non-Christian religions, an activity expressed through dialogue, contacts, prayer in common, investigation of the treasures of human spirituality, in which, as we know well, the members of these religions also are not lacking. Does it not sometimes happen that the firm belief of the followers of the non-Christian religions—a belief that is also an effect of the Spirit of truth operating outside the visible confines of the mystical body—can make Christians ashamed of being often themselves so disposed to doubt concerning the truths revealed by God and proclaimed by the Church . . .[26]

When is the time for the church to truly recognize and embrace what God and the Spirit make known in religions outside of our own? When is the time for us to allow what we discover about God in the religions outside of our own to edify our own understandings? When? Now.

What is needed in the church for us to continue the trajectory of positive advances in ecumenical and interreligious dialogue which view other religions as possible ways of salvation is for the church to continue to move beyond a juridical essentialistic approach to understanding itself and be open to a pastoral existential understanding. A juridical essentialistic approach tends to equate all ecclesial tradition with the apostolic tradition. It tends to view the church in terms of offices and structures in and of themselves, considering their respective juridical authority, and apart from the community of believers. A pastoral existential approach views apostolic

26. John Paul II, *Redemptor Hominis*, sec. 6.

tradition as a work of the Spirit, a dynamic process whereby each successive generation receives anew what was delivered to the apostolic community in a manner that pastorally resonates with the existing conditions of current time. It tends to view the church in terms of offices and structures and their respective juridical authority but does so vis-a-vis one another as well as vis-s-vis the *sensus fidelium*.[27]

The New Testament itself reveals that the apostolic tradition is a living process. Apostolic tradition is to be distinguished from the various theological, disciplinary, liturgical, or devotional traditions born in local churches over the centuries. These are particular forms, adapted to different places and times, in which the apostolic tradition is expressed. In light of apostolic tradition these other ecclesiastical traditions can be retained, modified, or even abandoned under the Spirit's guidance.[28] The creation of the apostolic tradition is the work of the Holy Spirit. Handing on this tradition is also the Spirit's work. It is a dynamic process in history whereby each successive generation is called to receive it as a gift from the Spirit. The Spirit also enables each successive generation of believers to respond to the gift and give it renewed expression to meet the needs of the pilgrim church as it unfolds in history. Understanding the difference between the apostolic tradition and the various ecclesiastical traditions is crucial in continuing the reform and renewal of the Roman Catholic Church and in progressing forward in the search for Christian unity.[29]

Revelation must be recalled in every new situation. Ecclesiastical traditions must be evaluated so as to discern their ongoing adequacy in new contexts.[30] The Christian community of each generation is called to receive the apostolic tradition anew through the assistance of the Holy

27. Throughout the book *sensus fidelium* has referred to what the Second Vatican Council referred to as the supernatural sense of the faith of the whole people of God; a gift of the Holy Spirit whereby the spirit arouses and sustains the faithful in their reception of the Word of God and their efforts to adhere to, penetrate, and apply said Word to daily life. *Sensus fidei* refers to this gift bestowed upon each individual baptized believer as a constitutive aspect of the gift of faith itself. *Consensus fidelium* refers to the end product of the process of determining the church's unified diversity of faith regarding a particular matter—it is a determination voiced by the magisterium but must be informed by the diverse *sensus fidelium* of the world church. See Ormand Rush, *Eyes of Faith*, 3–4, 242–4.

28. *Catechism of the Catholic Church*, 24–25.

29. Tkacik and McGonigle, *Pneumatic Correctives*, 125.

30. Anglican-Roman Catholic International Commission, *Authority in Church 2*, 21–22.

Spirit because of the changing needs of the church in diverse cultural situations and also because the church, as a community of frail human beings, is always in need of reform.[31] Fidelity to the Spirit in interpreting anew the apostolic tradition requires that the church heed what the Spirit communicates through all of its members, not just the clergy. As we saw in the third chapter, the church's charism of teaching is meant to be exercised by all the people of God who make up the body of Christ. Collectively, all the members of the church share in discerning what may be needed for the wellbeing and mission of the community, or when some element of ecclesiastical tradition needs to be received in a new way.[32] Hence, ecclesial authority needs to be exercised in a dialectical manner between clergy and laity and vis-à-vis other Christian religions. Ecclesial offices and juridical authority are to serve *koinonia* (communion). There is much still to be done to further the dialectic of mutuality that ought to exist between pope and the college of bishops, bishops among themselves, clergy vis-à-vis the laity, and Catholicism vis-à-vis other Christian brothers and sisters.

To continue to advance its fidelity to its mission to all people and commitment to dialoguing with the world's other non-Christian religions, the Catholic Church needs to embrace what Paul F. Knitter calls a "mutualist position." The church must not regard the Catholic/Christian religion as the one and only true faith and way of salvation. While holding firm to its own distinct identity, the church must recognize the distinct, valued identity of others without asserting that Catholicism/Christianity is the one supreme, normative, fulfilling, end-point religion for all others.[33] As we saw in Chapter Three, the Spirit of God is at work within other religions providing them grace, truth, goodness, and holiness.

According to Knitter, "To affirm pluralism is not to affirm relativism."[34] Dialogue represents a middle path between absolutism and relativism for all participants are committed to both witnessing their own truth as well as open to learning from the truth of others.[35] Such interreligious dialogue lends to mutual knowledge and enrichment while also allowing for mutual questioning.[36] "There is more truth in many religions than there can be in

31. Tkacik and McGonigle, *Pneumatic Correctives*, 129.

32. Anglican-Roman Catholic International Commission, *Authority in Church 2*, 24.

33. Knitter, "Bridge or Boundary," 262–263.

34. Knitter, "Bridge or Boundary," 264.

35. Knitter, "Bridge or Boundary," 264.

36. Knitter, "Bridge or Boundary," 266.

any one, Christianity included. . . . God's revelation through the Spirit in the religions cannot be reduced to what God has revealed in Jesus,"[37] Knitter maintains.

NON-ORDAINED—THE LAITY

Above and in Chapter Four we learned of the Christ-appointed and Spirit-endowed participation of the laity in the prophetic teaching office and kingly ministry of the church. The *sensus fidelium*, as an expression of the laity's sharing in the prophetic ministry of Jesus, is meant to serve as a pneumatic corrective which constantly renews the church's mission. As discussed in Chapter Four the church needs to develop institutional structures, mechanisms, and vehicles for the laity to exercise their prophetic and kingly roles *ad intra*. Laity and clergy alike have gifts for ecclesial governance. Parish and diocesan councils, diocesan synods, pastoral councils, parish-based councils and committees, and ecclesial tribunals are all recognized by the *Catechism of the Catholic Church* as appropriate vehicles for the laity and clergy to engage one another in the exercise of their respective gifts of authority.[38] When is the time for these vehicles to be more than consultative? When is the time for these vehicles to be permanent and not at the discretion of the clergy? When? Now.

In addition to the vehicles identified above the church needs to continue to advance the shift toward synodal ecclesial governance which has evolved in the decades since the Second Vatican Council. In light of the dominant expression of ecclesial self-understanding voiced at Vatican II which accentuated the church as the people of God, coupled with the Council's unprecedented consideration of the laity, de-centralized means of ecclesial governance which involve the laity are warranted. Such involvement of the laity and deference to the local churches recognize the primacy of the baptized and the Spirit's dynamic operation in the church. Synodality puts into practice the participative and collaborative process of church governance endorsed by Vatican II. A broader sense of synodality would recognize the place of all the faithful baptized in the prudential discernment of church governance and decision making. As a communion, all authority is meant to serve the community.[39]

37. Knitter, "Bridge or Boundary," 271–2.
38. *Catechism of the Catholic Church*, 240.
39. See Horan, "Synodality isn't just an option."

Citing the desire of God for the church of the twenty-first century and the process of renewal begun at the Second Vatican Council, Pope Francis initiated a two-year process in 2021 to eventuate in a synod on synodality. The universal church is to consider how greater communion can be achieved within the church so that greater participation among all of the faithful can contribute to the mission of the church. Grounded in the *sensus fidei* shared by all of the faithful, the process acknowledges that all of the faithful have a role to play in discerning God's call and in making pastoral decisions which correspond to the will of God for the church and which enable the church to provide a better witness of the gospel to the world. The process is to unfold in a manner whereby collective discernment and pastoral decisions emerge out of diocesan, regional, and continental efforts to eventuate in a universal synthesis.[40] Let us hope that this process truly does usher in a new era of shared ecclesial decision making and governance that enables the church to walk together with the Holy Spirit and to respect the baptismal dignity and charisms of all.

Synodality, de-centralization, and deference to local churches respects the consistent call for subsidiarity voiced in Catholic social teaching. Subsidiarity acknowledges and affirms that discerning what the Spirit is asking of the church in a particular time and place is best ascertained by the members in that particular community. It recognizes and affirms the competency and expertise of the ecclesial members at the local level. It defers to the decisions made at the local level. Hence, subsidiarity also advances the teachings regarding the local church, laity, and *sensus fidelium* espoused by Vatican II. Embracing the principle in praxis would require that Rome defer to regional bishops and national conferences, national conferences defer to diocesan bishops, and diocesan bishops defer to parishes in matters pertaining to ecclesial governance. It would require a *kenosis* of power throughout many levels of current church authority. And, it would require the church to accept unity unto diversity and plurality. When is the time for the baptismal dignity of the laity and corresponding appointments, apostolates, and charisms associated with it to be institutionally recognized in ways that are authentically substantive and authoritative? When is the time for synodality and subsidiarity in matters of ecclesial governance and decision making? When? Now.

It should be noted that the Catholic Church can learn much from our Protestant brothers and sisters in matters of lay participation, synodality,

40. See Synod 2021–2023.

and subsidiarity vis-à-vis ecclesial governance. Within the Evangelical Lutheran Church of America, ecclesial decision making is a process which involves parish-based consideration and vote, parish representation and voting at regional synods, and parish-based calls of clergy in cooperation with the bishop. Ecclesial decision making involves all members of the church, and ecclesial decisions are made through collegiality, cooperation, and collaboration. They are arrived at through consensus, not unilaterally imposed decisions proffered by clergy apart from the considerations and input of the laity.

Additionally, within the context of the American church, much could be learned from the form of governance which marks the American political experiment: separation of powers and representation. The Catholic Church could discern ways in which the pope, bishops, other clergy, and the laity each and all exercise power within the church and serve as mutual correctives to one another. Parishes could have lay representatives elected by the community who present the consensus of the parish to the diocese. The diocese, in turn, could have elected lay members as part of a representative body which informs the national episcopal conference and Vatican. Laity could hold positions of equal authority on parish, episcopal, and universal offices entrusted with ecclesial decision making, including Vatican curial offices and ecumenical councils.

Underlying the contemporary exclusion of the laity from substantive and authoritative vehicles and intruments of ecclesial governance and decision making, it must be said, is an unhealthy clericalism. Referring to clericalism as a scourge which places a caste of priests above the people of God,[41] Pope Francis has lamented as much:

> In some cases, it is because lay persons have not been given the formation needed to take on important responsibilities. In others, it is because in their particular churches room has not been made for them to speak and to act, due to an excessive clericalism which keeps them away from decision making.[42]
> A failure to realize that the mission belongs to the entire church, and not to the individual priest or bishop, limits the horizon, and even worse, stifles all the initiatives that the Spirit may be awakening in our midst. Let us be clear about this. The laypersons are not our peons, or our employees. They don't have to parrot back whatever we say. "Clericalism, far from giving impetus to various

41. Francis, "Deacons are the Guardians."
42. See Francis, *Evangelii Gaudium*, sec. 102.

contributions and proposals, gradually extinguishes the prophetic flame to which the entire Church is called to bear witness. Clerical-ism forgets that the visibility and the sacramentality of the Church belong to all the faithful people of God (*Lumen Gentium*, 9–14), not only to the few chosen and enlightened."[43]

As this book was being finalized, a diocese in Arizona deemed thou-sands of baptisms invalid because over the years of his ministry a presiding priest deviated from the prescribed baptismal formula: "I baptize you in the name of the…" Instead, he said, "We baptize you in the name of the…" The offending priest resigned from his parish ministry and is assisting the diocese in identifying those who may have been impacted for it has been determined that they must be baptized anew.[44]

Such a determination was informed, in part, due to a prevailing sense of holy orders which accentuates that the ordained is ontologically changed and is solely and exclusively able to act in the person of Jesus within the sacramental economy. Such clericalsism, in turn, informs an understand-ing that the ordained alone can be the person and voice of Jesus within the context of the sacrament. This in spite of the fact of what the Con-gregation for the Doctirne of Faith acknowledges, namely that baptism is a communal event,[45] that the baptized is baptized in lieu of the faith of the community, and that baptism unites one to the community—the com-munity which is understood to be the body of Christ. The Congregation's *Responses to questions proposed on the validity of baptism conferred with the formula, "We baptize you in the name of the Father and of the Son and of the Holy Spirit,"* maintains that when celebrating a sacrament the church in fact functions as the body that acts inseparably from its head. It is Christ the head who acts in the ecclesial body generated by him in the Paschal Mystery. It is Christ who acts in celebration of the sacraments. The subject is the church, the body of Christ together with its head, that manifests itself in the concrete gathered assembly. Nonetheless it also asserts that it is the ordained minister who is the "sign presence" of Jesus who calls the ecclesial community together and the one who ensures that the sacrament is not subject to arbitrariness.[46] In short, the Congregation's *Responses* ultimately posits that the ordained alone is capable of acting ministerially as "sign

43. Francis, "Meeting with the Bishops."
44. See Billeaud, "Priest's New Assignment."
45. See Tkacik and McGonigle, *Pnuematic Correctives.*
46. See Congregation Doctrine of Faith, *Responses Questions Validity Baptism.*

presence" of the person of Jesus and who ensures that a liturgical assembly is an expression of the real nature of the true church. Such is posited even as it is recognized that the community functions as the body of Christ, it is acknowledged that Jesus acts through the community, and that Christ is present in the concrete liturgical assembly (see above). Why, then, can it not be said that the community is acting in the person of Jesus within the celebration of baptism? According to the Congregation's "Responses," the utilization of "we" in the baptismal formula fails to honor that it is Jesus, himself, who baptizes in contrast to when baptism is conducted by a priest who utilizes the "I" formula.[47]

Here the failure to honor the laity's baptismal dignity and the continued subordination of the laity's participation in sacramental life is clearly illustrated. The laity continue to be treated as inferior to the clergy and relegated to a secondary status within the sacramental economy. When is the time for such clericalism to give way to the rightful affirmation of the laity's baptismal dignity and corresponding roles and responsibilities within the life of the church? When is it time for the lay members of the church to be acknowledged as constituting and functioning as the presence of Christ? When is it time for greater theological common sense and humility to recognize that Jesus communicating grace to human beings can be conducted communally as well as individually by one who is ordained? When is it time that such actions and powers of Jesus are not circumscribed by verbal formulations? When? Now.

COURAGE IN THE SPIRIT

Alfred Loisy once suggested that Jesus preached the kingdom of God and we ended up with the church. As the church discerns the questions regarding women, homosexuals, ecumenism (and interreligious dialogue), and the non-ordained (laity) in the life of its communities of faith today, courage from the Spirit will be required. The church may require the courage to change if it is to be faithful to the values of the kingdom of God. The church must have the courage to make mistakes along the way. Such courage is warranted for it is only if the church listens to what the Spirit is saying about these various issues that it can have the confidence that it is being faithful to its mission. Furthermore, if faithful to the Spirit, even if mistakes are made along the way, the Spirit will offer pneumatic correctives so as to

47. See Vatican News, "CDF: Baptisms Modified Formulas Not Valid."

redirect the church to what is being asked of it.[48] Time is of the essence for such ecclesial courage and change for former/fallen away Catholics is one of the fasting growing religious identifications in the United States.

In writing this book I needed courage from the Spirit. As stated at the beginning of this work, I love the church. I see my vocation as one in service to the church. I want the church to be the best it can be. It is my wish that I and the church be faithful to what the Spirit is saying so that the gospel message can be presented in ways that make known the love of God for all people. It is my wish that all people feel valued, respected, and welcomed in the church in ways that allow the gifts of the Spirit that each person has to be exercised for the building up of the church. If not now, when?

48. See Fielder and Rabben, *Rome Has Spoken.*

Bibliography

Alberigo, Giuseppe. *A Brief History of Vatican II*. Maryknoll, New York: Orbis, 2006.

Angelini, Giuseppe, "The *Sensus Fidelium* and Moral Discernment." In *The Sensus Fidelium and Moral Theology*, edited by Charles E. Curran and Lisa A. Fullam, 265. Mahwah, New Jersey: Paulist, 2017.

Anglican-Roman Catholic International Commission I. "Authority in the Church II." Windsor, 1981. Anglican-Roman Catholic Dialogue. https://iarccum.org/doc/?d=7.

Bellitto, Christopher M. *The General Councils: A History of the Twenty-One Church Councils from Nicea to Vatican II*. New York: Paulist, 2002.

Benedict XVI, Pope. *Deus Caritas Est* (God is Love). Papal Archive. The Holy See. 2006. https://www.vatican.va/content/benedict-xvi/en/encyclicals/documents/hf_ben-xvi_enc_20051225_deus-caritas-est.html.

Bevans, SVD, Stephen B. and Jeffrey Gros, FSC. *Rediscovering Vatican II: Evangelization and Religious Freedom*. New York: Paulist, 2009.

Bible.org. *Homosexuality: The Biblical Christian View*. https://bible.org/article/homosexuality-biblical-christian-view.

Billeaud, Jacques. "Priest's new assignment: Helping those he invalidly baptized." https://www.ncronline.org/news/parish/priests-new-assignment-helping-those-he-invalidly-baptized.

Birch, Bruce, and Larry Rasmussen. "The Use of the Bible in Christian Ethics." In *Introduction To Christian Ethics: A Reader*, edited by Ronald P. Hamel and Kenneth R. Himes, OFM, 322-332. Mahwah, New Jersey: Paulist, 1989.

Boff, Leonardo. *Ecclesiogenesis: The Base Communities Reinvent the Church*. Maryknoll, New York: Orbis, 1986.

Borg, Marcus J. *Meeting Jesus Again for the First Time*. San Francisco, California: Harper Collins, 1995.

Briggs, Ken. "Methodists may set agree to disagree model for churches in strife." https://www.ncronline.org/news/opinion/roundtable/methodists-may-set-agree-disagree-model-churches-strife.

Brown, SS, Raymond E. *An Introduction to New Testament Christology*. New York: Paulist, 1994.

———. *The Churches the Apostles Left Behind*. New York: Paulist, 1984.

Brown, SS, Raymond E., et al., eds. *The New Jerome Biblical Commentary*. New Jersey: Prentice Hall, 1990.

Burkhard, OFM Conv., John J. *Apostolicity Then and Now: An Ecumenical Church in a Postmodern World*. Collegeville, Minnesota: Liturgical, 2004.

————. "*Sensus Fidei*: Meaning, Role and Future of the Teaching of Vatican II." In *The Sensus Fidelium and Moral Theology*, edited by Charles E. Curran and Lisa A. Fullam, 87. Mahwah, New Jersey: Paulist, 2017.

Callan, Terrance. *The Origins of the Christian Faith*. New York: Paulist, 1994.

Cardman, Fracine. "One Treasure Only: Vatican II and the Ecumenical Nature of the Church." In *Vatican II: The Unfinished Agenda—A Look to The Future*, edited by Lucien Richard, OMI, et al, 176. New York: Paulist, 1987.

Cassidy, Edward Idris Cardinal. *Rediscovering Vatican II: Ecumenism and Interreligious Dialogue*. New York: Paulist, 2005.

Catechism of the Catholic Church. Washington, DC.: United States Catholic Conference, 1994.

Catholic Theological Society of America et al. *Human Sexuality: New Directions in American Catholic Thought*. New York: Paulist, 1977.

Chiu, Jose Enrigue Aguilar, et al., eds. *The Paulist Biblical Commentary*. New York: Paulist, 2018.

Cohen, Charles L., et al, eds. *The Future of Interreligious Dialogue: A Multireligious Conversation on Nostra Aetate*. Maryknoll, New York: Orbis, 2017.

Congar, OP, Yves. *Diversity and Communion*. Mystic, Connecticut: Twenty-Third, 1985.

————. *Divided Christendom*. London: Geoffrey Bles, 1939.

————. *I Believe in The Holy Spirit Volumes 1-3*. New York: Crossroad Herder, 1997.

————. *Lay People in The Church*. Westminster, Maryland: Christian Classics, 1985.

————. *Power and Poverty in the Church*. Baltimore, Maryland: Helicon, 1964.

————. *True And False Reform in The Church*. Collegeville, Minnesota: Liturgical, 2011.

Congregation for the Doctrine of Faith. *Inter Insigniores* (On the Question of Admission of Women to the Ministerial Priesthood). https://www.vatican.va/roman_curia/ congregations/cfaith/documents/rc_con_cfaith_doc_19761015_inter-insigniores_ en.html.

————. *Letter to the Bishops of the Catholic Church on the Collaboration of Men and Women in the Church and in the World*. http://www.va/roman_curia/congregations/ cfaith/documents/rc_con_cfaith_doc_20040731collaboration_en.html.

————. *Letter to the Bishops of the Catholic Church on the Pastoral Care of Homosexual Persons*. http//www.vatican.va/roman_curia/congregations/cfaith/documents/rc_ con_cfaith_doc_19861001 homosexual-persons_en.html.

————. *Responses to Questions Proposed on the Validity of Baptism Conferred with the Formula, "We baptize you in the name of the Father and of the Son and of the Holy Spirit."* https://press.vatican.va/content/salastampa/it/bollettino/pubblico/2020/08/06/ 0406/00923.html#rispostein.

Congregation for the Doctrine of Faith et al. *Instruction on Certain Questions Regarding the Collaboration of the Non-Ordained Faithful in the Sacred Ministry of Priest*. https://www.vatican.va/roman_curia/pontifical_councils/laity/documents/rc_con_ interdic_doc_15081997_en.html.

Crowley, SJ, Paul G. "Catholicity, Inculturation, and Newman's *Sensus Fidelium*." In *The Sensus Fidelium and Moral Theology*, edited by Charles E. Curran and Lisa A. Fullam, 66. Mahwah, New Jersey: Paulist, 2017.

Curran, Charles E. *Catholic Moral Theology in the United States: A History*. Washington, D.C.: Georgetown University, 2009

————. *Contemporary Problems in Moral Theology*. Notre Dame, Indiana: Fides, 1970.

———. "Natural Law and Contemporary Moral Theology." In Charles E. Curran, *Contemporary Problems in Moral Theology*, 97-158. Notre Dame, Indiana: Fides Publishers, 1970.

———. *Roman Catholic Sexual Ethics: A Dissenting View*. Religion Online, December 16, 1987. https://www.religion-online.org/article/roman-catholic-sexual-ethics-a-dissenting-view/.

———. *Readings in Moral Theology No. 3: The Magisterium and Morality*. New York: Paulist, 1982.

Curran, Charles E. and Lisa A. Fullam, eds. *The Sensus Fidelium and Moral Theology*. New York: Paulist, 2017.

Curran, Charles E. and Richard A. McCormick, SJ, eds. *John Paul II and Moral Theology*. New York: Paulist, 1998.

Davis, Leo Donald. *The First Seven Ecumenical Councils (325-787): Their History and Theology*. Collegeville, Minnesota: Liturgical, 1983.

DeBernardo, Francis. "From 'Who Am I to Judge' to 'God Made You Like This and Loves You Like This.'" https://www.newwaysministry.org/2018/05/22/from-who-am-i-to-judge-to-god-made-you-like-this-and-loves-you-like-this/.

———. "On Flight Back to Rome, Pope Francis Offers Advice to Parents of Lesbian and Gay People." https://www.newwaysministry.org/2018/08/27/on-flight-back-to-rome-pope-francis-offers-advice-to-parents-of-lesbian-and-gay-people/.

———. "The Many Faces of Pope Francis: A Timeline of His LGBTQ Record." March 13, 2018. https://www.newwaysministry.org/2018/03/13/many-faces-pope-francis-five-year-timeline-lgbt-record/.

de Vogue, Ariane and Devin Cole. "Supreme Court says Federal Law Protects LGBTQ Workers from Discrimination." https://www.cnn.com/2020/06/15/politics/supreme-court-lgbtq-employment-case/index.html.

Dulles, Avery Cardinal. *Models of the Church*. New York: Doubleday, 2002.

Epko, Anthony. "The *Sensus Fidelium* and the Threefold Office of Christ: A Reinterpretation of *Lumen Gentium* No. 12." In *The Sensus Fidelium and Moral Theology*, edited by Charles E. Curran and Lisa A. Fullam. 82-84. Mahwah, New Jersey: Paulist, 2017.

Evans, Rachel Held. *Wholehearted Faith*. New York: Harper One, 2021.

Faggioli, Massimo. *Vatican II: The Battle for Meaning*. New York: Paulist, 2012.

Feldmeier, Peter. *Encounters in Faith: Christianity in Interreligious Dialogue*. Winona, Minnesota: Anselm Academic, 2011.

Fielder, Maureen and Linda Rabben. *Rome Has Spoken . . .* New York: Crossroad, 1998.

Fiorenza, Elisabeth Schussler. *In Memory of Her*. New York: Crossroad, 1994.

Flannery, O.P., Austin, ed. *Vatican Council II: The Conciliar and Post Conciliar Documents*. New York: Costello, 1998.

Ford, Jr., Craig A. *A Natural Law for Queer and Racial Justice*. January 21, 2020. https://canopyforum.org/2020/01/21/a-natural-law-for-queer-and-racial-justice-by-craig-ford/.

———. *Church Teaching on Sexuality and Gender Must Reflect LGBT People's Realities, says Theologian*. January 5, 2019. https://www.newwaysministry.org/2019/01/05/church-teaching-on-sexuality-and-gender-must-reflect-lgbt-peoples-realities-says-theologian/.

———. "LGBT Catholics Are a Reality." *Commonweal*, December 19, 2018. https://www.commonwealmagazine.org/lgbt-catholics-are-reality.

————. *The Complicity of Catholic Progressives in Amoris Laetitia Commentary.* May 13, 2016. https://catholicmoraltheology.com/the-complicity- of-of-catholic-progressives-in-amoris-laetitia-commentary/.

Fox, Thomas C. *Curran: Papacy should admit some of its teachings are wrong.* November 21, 2014. https://www.ncronline.org/news/accountability/curran-papacy-should-admit-some-its-teachings-are-wrong.

Fraga, Brian. "Marquette Diocese's LGBTQ restrictions blasted as cruel policy." https://www.ncronline.org/news/marquette-dioceses-lgbtq-restrictions-blasted-cruel-policy.

Francis, Pope. *Amoris Laetitia* (On Love in the Family). https://www.vatican.va/content/dam/francesco/pdf/apost_exhortations/documents/papa-francesco_esortazione-ap_20160319_amoris-laetitia_en.pdf.

————. *Christus Vivit* (Christ is Alive). https://www.vatican.va/content/francesco/en/apost_exhortations/documents/papa-francesco_esortazione-ap_20190325_christus-vivit.html.

————. "Deacons are the Guardians of Service in the Church." https://www.catholicculture.org/culture/library/view.cfm?recnum=12533.

————. *Evangelii Gaudium* (The Joy of the Gospel). https://www.vatican.va/content/francesco/en/apost_exhortations/documents/papa-francesco_esortazione-ap_20131124_evangelii-gaudium.html.

————. "Meeting with the Bishops: Apostolic Journey of His Holiness Pope Francis to Chile and Peru (15-22 January 2018)". https://www.vatican.va/content/francesco/en/speeches/2018/january/documents/papa-francesco_20180116_cile-santiago-vescovi.html.

————. *Querida Amazonia* (Beloved Amazon). http://www.vatican.va/content/francesco/en/apost_exhortations/documents/papa-francesco_esortazione-ap_20200202_querida-amazonia.html.

Freyne, Sean. "The Bible and Christian Morality," In *Introduction To Christian Ethics: A Reader,* edited by Ronald P. Hamel and Kenneth R. Himes, O.F.M, 9-32. Mahwah, New Jersey: Paulist, 1989.

Gaillardetz, Richard R. *Rediscovering Vatican II: The Church in the Making.* New York: Paulist, 2006.

Gaillardetz, Richard R. and Catherine E. Clifford. *Keys to the Council: Unlocking the Teaching of Vatican II.* Collegeville, Minnesota: Liturgical, 2012.

Gibson, David. "Miami archbishop warns employees against expressing support for gay marriage." https://www.ncronline.org/news/parish/miami-archbishop-warns-employees-against-expressing-support-gay-marriage?site_redirect=1.

Gorski, Eugene F. *Theology of Religions: A Sourcebook for Interreligious Study.* New York: Paulist, 2008.

Grecco, Richard. "Recent Ecclesiastical Teaching." In *John Paul II and Moral Theology,* edited by Charles E. Curran and Richard A. McCormick, SJ., 138 and 153. Mahwah, New Jersey: Paulist, 1998.

Gula, SS, Richard M. "Human Person." In *Reason Informed by Faith: Foundations of Catholic Morality,* 165-184. Mahwah, New Jersey: Paulist, 1989.

————. "Moral Decision Making." In *Reason Informed by Faith: Foundations of Catholic Morality,* 165-184. Mahwah, New Jersey: Paulist, 1989.

————. "Natural Law in Tradition." In *Reason Informed by Faith: Foundations of Catholic Morality,* 165-184. Mahwah, New Jersey: Paulist, 1989.

———. "Natural Law Today." In *Reason Informed by Faith: Foundations of Catholic Morality*, 165-184. Mahwah, New Jersey: Paulist, 1989.

———. *Reason Informed by Faith: Foundations of Catholic Morality*, 165-184. Mahwah, New Jersey: Paulist, 1989.

———. "Scripture in Moral Theology." In *Reason Informed by Faith: Foundations of Catholic Morality*, 165-184. Mahwah, New Jersey: Paulist, 1989.

Hamel, Ronald P. and Kenneth R. Himes, OFM, eds. *Introduction to Christian Ethics: A Reader*. New York: Paulist, 1989.

Hansen, Luke. "Top Five Takeaways from the Amazon Synod." https://www.americamagazine.org/faith/2019/11/11/top-five-takeaways-amazon-synod.

Heft, James, ed. *After Vatican II: Trajectories and Hermeneutics*. Grand Rapids, Michigan: Eerdmans, 2012.

Helminiak, Daniel A. *The Same Jesus: A Contemporary Christology*. Chicago: Loyola University, 1986.

Himes, Michael J. "The Human Person in Contemporary Theology: From Human Nature to Authentic Subjectivity." In *Introduction To Christian Ethics: A Reader*, edited by Ronald P. Hamel and Kenneth R. Himes, OFM, 49-62. Mahwah, New Jersey: Paulist, 1989.

Horan, Daniel P. "History will judge the church harshly for its treatment of LGBT persons." https://www.ncronline.org/news/opinion/history-will-judge-church-harshly-its-treatment-lgbtq-persons.

———. "Synodality isn't just an option, it's the only way to be church." https://www.ncronline.org/news/opinion/faith-seeking-understanding/synodality-isnt-just-option-its-only-way-be-church.

The House of Bishops of the Church of England, *May They All Be One: A Response to Ut Unum Sint*. 19-20. London: Church House, 1997.

International Theological Commission. *From the Diakonia of Christ to the Diakonia of the Apostles*. http://www.vatican.va/roman_curia/congregations/cfaith/cti_documents/rc_con_cfaith_pro_05072004_diaconate_en.html.

———. *Sensus Fidei in the Life of the Church*. http://www.vatican.va/roman_curia/congregations/cfaith/cti_documents/rc_cti_20140610_sensus-fidei_en.html.

"Isaiah." In *The Catholic Study Bible*, edited by Donald Senior. New York: Oxford University, 1990.

John XXIII, Pope. *Mater et Magistra* (On Christianity and Social Progress). https://www.vatican.va/content/john-xxiii/en/encyclicals/documents/hf_j-xxiii_enc_15051961_mater.html.

John Paul II, Pope. *Centesimus Annus* (On the Hundredth Anniversary of *Rerum Novarum*). https://www.vatican.va/content/john-paul-ii/en/encyclicals/documents/hf_jp-ii_enc_01051991_centesimus-annus.html.

———. *Christifideles Laici* (On the Vocation and the Mission of the Lay Faithful in the Church and in the World). https://www.vatican.va/content/john-paul-ii/en/apost_exhortations/documents/hf_jp-ii_exh_30121988_christifideles-laici.html.

———. *Dives in Misericordia* (Rich in Mercy). https://www.vatican.va/content/john-paul-ii/en/encyclicals/documents/hf_jp-ii_enc_30111980_dives-in-misericordia.html.

———. *Dominum Et Vivificantem* (On the Holy Spirit in the Life of the Church and the World). https://www.vatican.va/content/john-paul-ii/en/encyclicals/documents/hf_jp-ii_enc_18051986_dominum-et-vivificantem.html.

———. *Ex Corde Ecclesia* (From the Heart of the Church). https://www.vatican.va/content/john-paul-ii/en/apost_constitutions/documents/hf_jp-ii_apc_15081990_ex-corde-ecclesiae.html.

———. *Familiaris Consortio* (On the Role of the Christian Family in the Modern World). https://www.vatican.va/content/john-paul-ii/en/apost_exhortations/documents/hf_jp-ii_exh_19811122_familiaris-consortio.html.

———. *Mulieris Dignitatem* (On the Dignity and Vocation of Women). http://www.vatican.va/content/john-paul-ii/en/apost_letters/1988/documents/hf_jp-ii_apl_19880815_mulieris-dignitatem.html.

———. *Ordinatio Sacerdotalis* (On Reserving Priestly Ordination to Men Alone). http://w2.vatican.va/content/john-paul-ii/en/apost_letters/1994/documents/hf_jp-ii_apl_19940522_ordinatio-sacerdotalis.html.

———.*Redemptor Hominis* (The Redeemer of Man). https://www.vatican.va/content/john-paul-ii/en/encyclicals/documents/hf_jp-ii_enc_04031979_redemptor-hominis.html.

———.*Redemptoris Missio* (On the Permanent Validity of the Church's Missionary Mandate). https://www.vatican.va/content/john-paul-ii/en/encyclicals/documents/hf_jp-ii_enc_07121990_redemptoris-missio.html.

———. *Tertio Millennio Adveniente* (On Preparation for the Jubilee Year 200). https://www.vatican.va/content/john-paul-ii/en/apost_letters/1994/documents/hf_jp-ii_apl_19941110_tertio-millennio-adveniente.html.

———. *Ut Unum Sint* (That They Be One). http://www.vatican.va/content/john-paul-ii/en/encyclicals/documents/hf_jp-ii_enc_25051995_ut-unum-sint.html.

Johnson, Elizabeth A. *She Who Is*. New York: Crossroad, 2017.

Kelley, J.N.D. *Early Christian Doctrines*. Peabody, Massachusetts: Prince, 2007.

King, Jr., Martin Luther. "Letter from Birmingham Jail." https://kinginstitute.stanford.edu/sites/mlk/files/letterfrombirmingham_wwcw_0.pdf.

———. *Why We Can't Wait*. New York: Penguin, 1964.

Knitter, Paul. "Bridge or Boundary? Vatican II and Other Religions." In *Vatican II Forty Years Later* edited by William Madges, 261. Maryknoll, New York: Orbis, 2006.

———. "*Nostra Aetate*: A Milestone in the History of Religions? From Competition to Cooperation." In *The Future of Interreligious Dialogue: A Multi-Religious Dialogue on Nostra Aetate,* edited by Charles L. Cohen et al. Maryknoll, New York: Orbis, 2017.

Kung, Hans. *Reforming the Church Today*. London: T & T Clark, 2000.

———.*The Church*. New York: Sheed and Ward, 1967.

Last, Carl A., ed. *Remembering The Future: Vatican II and Tomorrow's Liturgical Agenda*. Mahwah, New Jersey: Paulist Press, 1983.

Leckey, Dolores R. *Rediscovering Vatican II: The Laity and Christian Education*. New York: Paulist, 2006.

Lee, Randall and Jeffrey Gros, FSC, eds. *The Church as Koinonia Of Salvation: Lutheran And Catholics In Dialogue X*. Washington, D.C.: Untied States Conference of Catholic Bishops, 2005.

"Leviticus." In *The Catholic Study Bible,* edited by Donald Senior. New York: Oxford University, 1990.

LGBTQ Catholics of Tampa Bay. "New Announcement."http://www.gaycatholicstampabay.com/.

Lombardi, Josephine. *What Are They Saying About the Universal Salvific Will of God?* New York: Paulist, 2008.

"Luke." In *The Catholic Study Bible*, edited by Donald Senior. New York: Oxford University, 1990.

Lynch, Bishop Robert. "It is religion, including our own which targets LGBT people." https://www.tampabay.com/news/religion/bishop-robert-lynch-it-is-religion-including-our-own-which-targets-lgbt/2281687/.

Madges, William, ed. *Vatican II Forty Years Later*. Maryknoll, New York: Orbis, 2006.

Madigan, Kevin and Carolyn Osiek, eds. *Ordained Women in the Early Church: A Documentary History*. Baltimore, Maryland: John Hopkins University, 2005.

Martin, S.J., James. *Building A Bridge: How the Catholic Church and the LGBT Community Can Enter into a Relationship of Respect, Compassion and Sensitivity*. New York: Harper One, 2017.

———. *We need to build a bridge between LGBT community and the Catholic Church*. *America*, October 30, 2016. https://www.americamagazine.org/faith/2016/10/30/james-martin-sj-we-need-build-bridge-between-lgbt-community-and-catholic-church.

———. "What is the official church teaching on homosexuality? Responding to a commonly asked question." *America*, April 30, 2018. https://www.americamagazine.org/faith/2018/04/06/what-official-church-teaching-homosexuality-responding-commonly-asked-question.

"Matthew." In *The Catholic Study Bible*, edited by Donald Senior. New York: Oxford University, 1990.

Mayer, Lawrence S. and Paul R. McHugh. *Sexuality and Gender: Findings from the Biological, Psychological and Social Sciences*. Danville, New Jersey: *The New Atlantis* Number 50, Fall 2016.

McBrien, Richard P. *The Church: The Evolution of Catholicism*. New York: Harper Collins, 2008.

McCann, Pamela, "Karl Rahner and the *Sensus Fidelium*." In *The Sensus Fidelium and Moral Theology*, edited by Charles E. Curran and Lisa A. Fullam, 164-187. Mahwah, New Jersey: Paulist, 2017.

McElwee, Joshua J. "Francis explains "who am I to judge?" https://www.ncronline.org/news/vatican/francis-explains-who-am-i-judge.

Modras, Ronald. "Pope John Paul II's Theology of the Body." In *John Paul II and Moral Theology*, edited by Charles E. Curran and Richard A. McComick, SJ, 150. Mahwah, New Jersey: Paulist, 1998.

Nachrichten-Agentur, Katholische. "Top EU cardinal calls for change in church teaching on gay relationships." https://www.ncronline.org/news/quick-reads/top-eu-cardinal-calls-change-church-teaching-gay-relationships.

National Catholic Reporter Editorial Staff. "The pope is NOT upset with Fr. James Martin." https://www.ncronline.org/news/opinion/editorial-pope-not-upset-fr-james-martin.

Newman, John Henry. *On Consulting the Faithful in Matters of Doctrine*. http://www.newmanreader.org/works/rambler/consulting.htm.

Neuner SJ, J. and J. Dupuis, SJ, eds. *The Christian Faith: Doctrinal Documents of the Catholic Church*. New York: Alba House, 1990.

Nguyen, Bishop Vincent Long Van. "Bishop Long, OFM Conv delivers 2016 Ann D Clark Lecture." https://catholicoutlook.org/bishop-vincent-long-ofm-conv-delivers-2016-ann-d-clark-lecture/.

Niebuhr, H. Richard. *Christ and Culture*. New York: Harper and Row, 1951.

O' Collins SJ, Gerald. *Christology: A Biblical, Historical and Systematic Study of Jesus.* New York: Oxford University, 2005.

———. *The Second Vatican Council on Other Religions.* New York: Oxford University Press, 2013.

O'Malley, John W. et al. *Vatican II: Did Anything Happen?* New York: Continuum International, 2007.

Origen. "Commentary on Romans 10:17." In Zagano, Phyllis, *Holy Saturday: An Argument for the Restoration of the Female Diaconate in the Catholic Church.* New York: Crossroad, 2002.

Paul VI, Pope. *Evangelii Nuntiandi* (Evangelization in the Modern World). https://www.vatican.va/content/paul-vi/en/apost_exhortations/documents/hf_p-vi_exh_19751208_evangelii-nuntiandi.html.

———. *Octogesima Adveniens* (On the Eightieth Anniversary of *Rerum Novarum*). https://www.vatican.va/content/paul-vi/en/apost_letters/documents/hf_p-vi_apl_19710514_octogesima-adveniens.html.

Pius XI, Pope. *Quadragesimo Anno* (On Reconstruction of the Social Order). https://www.vatican.va/content/pius-xi/en/encyclicals/documents/hf_p-xi_enc_19310515_quadragesimo-anno.html.

———. *Sacramentum Ordinis* (On the Sacrament of Orders). https://www.papalencyclicals.net/pius12/p12sacrao.htm.

Pontifical Council for Interreligious Dialogue. https://www.vatican.va/content/romancuria/en/pontifici-consigli/pontificio-consiglio-per-il-dialogo-interreligioso.index.html.

Pontifical Council for Promoting Christian Unity. https://www.vatican.va/content/romancuria/en/pontifici-consigli/pontificio-consiglio-per-la-promozione-dellunita-dei-cristiani.index.html.

———. *Directory for the Application of Principles and Norms on Ecumenism.* March 25, 1993. http://www.vatican.va/roman_curia/pontificalcouncils/chrstuni/documents/rc_pc_chrstunidoc25031993_principles-and-norms-on-ecumenism_en.html.

Pontifical Council for Promoting Christian Unity, and The Lutheran World Federation. *From Conflict to Communion.* https://www.lutheranworld.org/sites/default/files/From%20Conflict%20to%20Communion.pdf.

"Psalms." In *The Catholic Study Bible,* edited by Donald Senior. New York: Oxford University, 1990.

Rademacher, William J. *Lay Ministry: A Theological, Spiritual and Pastoral Handbook.* New York: Crossroad, 1992.

Rahner, Karl. *The Content of Faith.* New York: Crossroad, 1992.

Richard, OMI, Lucien et al., eds. *Vatican II: The Unfinished Agenda—A Look to the Future.* New York: Paulist, 1987.

Roberts, Judy. "Father James Martin Explains His Vision Regarding LGBT Catholics." *National Catholic Register,* July 10, 2017. https://www.ncregister.com/daily-news/father-james-martin-explains-his-vision-regarding-lgbt-catholics.

Rocca, Francis X. "German Catholic Leaders Support Blessings for Gay Couples, Challenging Pope Francis." https://www.wsj.com/articles/german-catholic-leaders-support-blessings-for-gay-couples-challenging-pope-francis-11633107983.

"Romans." In *The Catholic Study Bible,* edited by Donald Senior. New York: Oxford University, 1990.

Ryan, OP, Columba. "The Traditional Concept of Natural Law." In *Introduction To Christian Ethics: A Reader,* edited by Ronald P. Hamel and Kenneth R. Himes, OFM, 413-427. Mahwah, New Jersey: Paulist, 1989.

Rush, Ormand. *The Eyes of Faith: The Sense of the Faithful and the Church's Reception of Revelation.* Washington, D.C.: Catholic University of America, 2009.

———. *The Vision of Vatican II: Its Fundamental Principles.* Collegeville, Minnesota: Liturgical, 2019.

Schillebeeckx, OP, Edward. *Christ The Sacrament of the Encounter with God.* Kansas City, Missouri: Sheed and Ward, 1963.

———. *The Church with a Human Face: A New and Expanded Theology of Ministry.* New York: Crossroad, 1987.

Seasoltz, OSB, Kevin R. "The Sacred Liturgy: Development and Directions." In *Remembering The Future: Vatican II and Tomorrow's Liturgical Agenda,* edited by Carl A. Last. Mahwah, New Jersey: Paulist Press, 1983.

Sellner, Edward C. "Lay Spirituality," In *The Eyes of Faith: The Sense of the Faithful and the Church's Reception of Revelation,* Ormand Rush, 252. Washington, D.C.: Catholic University of America, 2009.

Senior, Donald and John J. Collins, eds. *The Catholic Study Bible.* New York: Oxford University, 2006.

Shine, Robert. "There is No Place for Homophobia, Pope Francis Told Gay Former Student." https://www.newwaysministry.org/2016/11/01/there-is-no-place-for-homophobia -pope-francis-told-gay-former-student/.

———. "Pope Francis Meets with LGBT Pilgrims as Sixth Anniversary of His Election Approaches." https://www.newwaysministry.org/2019/03/12/pope-francis-meets- with-lgbt-pilgrims-as-sixth-anniversary-of-his-election-approaches/.

Sisters of Charity of New York. "Leadership Team Shares Concerns with Cardinal Dolan." https://scny.org/leadership-team-shares-concerns-with-cardinal-dolan/.

Soede, Nathanael Yaovi, "The *Sensus Fidelium* and Moral Discernment: The Principle of Inculturation and of Love." In *The Sensus Fidelium and Moral Theology* edited by Charles E. Curran and Lisa A. Fullam, 229-233. Mahwah, New Jersey: Paulist, 2017.

Spohn, SJ, William. "What Are They Saying About Scripture and Ethics," In *Introduction to Christian Ethics: A Reader,* edited by Ronald P. Hamel and Kenneth R. Himes, OFM, 313-321. Mahwah, New Jersey: Paulist, 1989.

Sullivan, S.J., Francis A. *Magisterium: Teaching Authority In The Catholic Church.* New York: Paulist, 1983.

———."Vatican II and the Postconciliar Magisterium on the Salvation of Adherents of Other Religions." In *After Vatican II: Trajectories and Hermeneutics,* edited by James Heft. Grand Rapids, Michigan: Eerdmans, 2012.

Synod 2021-2023. https://www.synod.va/en.html.

Tanner, Norman. *Rediscovering Vatican II: The Church and the World.* New York: Paulist, 2005.

Taylor, Barbara Brown. *Holy Envy: Finding God in the Faith of Others.* New York: Harper Collins, 2019.

Tillard, OP, J.M.R. "Sensus Fidelium." In *The Sensus Fidelium and Moral Theolog,y* edited by Charles E. Curran and Lisa A. Fullam, 32 and 49. Mahwah, New Jersey: Paulist, 2017.

Tkacik, Michael J. *Deacons and Vatican II: The Making of a Servant Church.* Eugene, Oregon: Wipf and Stock, 2018.

Tkacik, Michael J. and Thomas C. McGonigle, O.P. *Pneumatic Correctives: What is the Spirit Saying to the Church of the 21st Century?* Lanham, Maryland: University Press of America, 2007.

United States Conference of Catholic Bishops. *Always Our Children.* https://www.usccb. org/resources/Always%20Our%20Children.pdf.

———. *Called and Gifted.* https://www.usccb.org/about/laity-marriage-family-life-and-youth/laity/upload/called_and_gifted.pdf.

———. *Co-Workers in the Vineyard of the Lord.* https://www.usccb.org/upload/co-workers-vineyard-lay-ecclesial-ministry-2005.pdf.

———. *From Words to Deeds.* https://www.usccb.org/committees/laity-marriage-family-life-youth/words-deeds.

———. *Ministry to Persons with a Homosexual Inclination: Guidelines for Pastoral Care.* https://www.usccb.org/resources/ministry-to-persons-of-homosexual-inclination _0.pdf.

United States Conference of Catholic Bishops Committee on Ecumenical and Interreligious Affairs and The Evangelical Lutheran Church in America. *Declaration on the Way.* https://download.elca.org/ELCA%20Resource%20Repository/Declaration_on_ the_Way.pdf.

Vagaggini, Cipriano. *Ordination Of Women to the Diaconate In The Eastern Churches.* Collegeville, Minnesota: Liturgical, 2013.

Valkenberg, Pim, ed. *World Religions in Dialogue: A Comparative Theological Approach.* Winona, Minnesota: Anselm Academic, 2013.

Vatican II Council. "*Ad Gentes Divinitus*: Decree on Missionary Activity." In *Vatican Council II: Volume 1 The Conciliar and Post Conciliar Documents,* edited by Austin Flannery, OP. Northport, New York: Costello, 1998.

Vatican II Council. "*Christus Dominus*: Decree on the Pastoral Office of the Bishops in the Church." In *Vatican Council II: Volume 1 The Conciliar and Post Conciliar Documents,* edited by Austin Flannery, OP. Northport, New York: Costello, 1998.

Vatican II Council. "*Dei Verbum*: Dogmatic Constitution on Divine Revelation." In *Vatican Council II: Volume 1 The Conciliar and Post Conciliar Documents,* edited by Austin Flannery, OP. Northport, New York: Costello, 1998.

Vatican II Council. "*Dignitatis Humanae*: Declaration on Religious Liberty." In *Vatican Council II: Volume 1 The Conciliar and Post Conciliar Documents,* edited by Austin Flannery, OP. Northport, New York: Costello, 1998.

Vatican II Council. "*Gaudium et Spes*: The Pastoral Constitution on the Church in the Modern World." In *Vatican Council II: Volume 1 The Conciliar and Post Conciliar Documents,* edited by Austin Flannery, OP. Northport, New York: Costello, 1998.

Vatican II Council. "*Gravissimum Educationis*: Declaration on Christian Education." In *Vatican Council II: Volume 1 The Conciliar and Post Conciliar Documents,* edited by Austin Flannery, OP. Northport, New York: Costello, 1998.

Vatican II Council. "*Lumen Gentium*: Dogmatic Constitution on the Church." In *Vatican Council II: Volume 1 The Conciliar and Post Conciliar Documents,* edited by Austin Flannery, OP. Northport, New York: Costello, 1998.

Vatican II Council. "*Nostra Aetate*: Declaration on the Relations of the Church to Non-Christian Religions." In *Vatican Council II: Volume 1 The Conciliar and Post Conciliar Documents,* edited by Austin Flannery, OP. Northport, New York: Costello, 1998.

Vatican II Council. "*Presbyterorum Ordinis*: Decree on the Ministry and Life of Priests" In *Vatican Council II: Volume 1 The Conciliar and Post Conciliar Documents,* edited by Austin Flannery, OP. Northport, New York: Costello, 1998.

Vatican II Council. "*Sacrosanctum Concilium*: The Constitution on the Sacred Liturgy." In *Vatican Council II: Volume 1 The Conciliar and Post Conciliar Documents,* edited by Austin Flannery, OP. Northport, New York: Costello, 1998.

Vatican II Council. "*Unitatis Redintegratio*: Decree on Ecumenism." In *Vatican Council II: Volume 1 The Conciliar and Post Conciliar Documents,* edited by Austin Flannery, OP. Northport, New York: Costello, 1998.

Vatican Commission for Religious Relations with the Jews. http://www.christianunity. va/content/unitacristiani/en/commissione-per-i-rapporti-religiosi-con-l-ebraismo/ commissione-per-i-rapporti-religiosi-con-l-ebraismo-crre.html.

Vatican Congregations. *Instruction on Certain Questions Regarding the Collaboration of the Non-Ordained Faithful in the Sacred Ministry of Priest.* August 15, 1997. https:// www.vatican.va/roman_curia/congregations/cclergy/documents/rc_con_interdic_ doc_15081997_en.html.

Vatican News, "CDF: Baptisms conferred with arbitrality modified formulas are not valid," August 6, 2020, at https://www.vaticannews.va/en/vatican-city/news/2020- 08/cdf-baptisms-with-arbitrarily-modified-formulas-are-not-valid.html.

Veliko, Lydia and Jeffrey Gros, FSC, eds. *Growing Consensus II: Church Dialogues in The United States, 1992-2004.* Washington, D.C.: United States Conference of Catholic Bishops, 2005.

Viladesau, Richard and Mark Massa. *World Religions: A Sourcebook for Students of Christian Theology.* New York: Paulist, 1994.

Wijlens, Myriam, "*Sensus Fidelium*—Authority Protecting and Promoting the Ecclesiology of Vatican II with the Assistance of Institutions?" In *The Sensus Fidelium and Moral Theology,* edited by Charles E. Curran and Lisa A. Fullam, 113-138. Mahwah, New Jersey: Paulist, 2017.

Witherup, Ronald D. *Rediscovering Vatican II: Scripture.* New York: Paulist, 2006.

Zagano, Phyllis. *Holy Saturday: An Argument for the Restoration of the Female Diaconate in the Catholic Church.* New York: Crossroad, 2002.

Lightning Source UK Ltd.
Milton Keynes UK
UKHW022028230822
407726UK00008B/1718